JESUS, RWANDA, AND GOSPEL LOVE

GARY W. MOORE

Publisher's Name: Gary w. Moore

ISBN: 978-1-968442-16-3

Table of Contents

INTRODUCTION

God loves you! Have you ever heard anyone say that to you? If you have been around the church during your journey, you have probably heard the phrase many times. So, if you have heard it many times or perhaps have never heard it, as you read it now, what does it mean to you? I have been in ministry as a pastor, missionary, and denominational leader for over five decades and I have heard many responses and definitions given to that phrase: God loves you! However, I have come to the conclusion that most of them were **wrong!** Now, that is a bold, perhaps even audacious statement, and I agree. It is not that the definitions or even the applications to that phrase were or are wrong, rather it is the foundation that does not allow us to fully build on the awesome, unconditional, unfailing, lavishing love of God.

Have you ever ridden on a railroad train? My wife, LaVonna, and I were privileged to ride on the TGV, the high speed train in France, from Paris to Montpelier. By car, it is an eight hour journey, but on the TGV it took only three hours. It was like we were riding on air and when we looked out the window at the countryside, we had to look somewhere in the distance, because the speed was so great, if we looked close to the train it was just a blur. As we consider the love of God, I would like us to think of a railroad track. There are two tracks, and they have to be going in the exact same direction in order for the train to ride on them. Let's think of them as definition and direction.

What is the definition of love? Webster's dictionary states that love is a "strong affection for another arising out of kinship or personal ties". An additional definition is "an attraction based on sexual desire: affection and tenderness felt by lovers." Every definition of love is centered around attraction, feelings, emotions, affections, and the expressions of such things. We have multitudes of stories, books, songs, poems, plays, and movies that are centered around these themes, all in the name of love. So, when we hear or see the words, God loves you, what do we think? We naturally think in the context of the above definitions and expressions. Is that wrong? Well, it may not be wrong, but it is not right. How can that be? The Bible uses multiple words that we translate into English as "love". The New Testament was originally written in the Greek language and there were two words that are both translated into "love" in English. Those words are *agape* and *fileo*. The word *eros*, from which we derive the word "erotic" was used in Greek culture at the time, but is not used in the New Testament. The word *fileo* is a very strong word as it denotes deep friendship and affection, much as we think of the word love. All of the meanings that we saw in the definitions above are included in the meaning of *fileo*. While it appears that there are times when *fileo* and *agape* seem to be used interchangeably, there is a fundamental difference that is very difficult for us to comprehend and thus build our concepts, expressions, and experiences of love on the proper foundation. In 1 John 4:7 we read "for love comes from God". A few verses later, verse 10, it states "This is love: not that we loved God, but that he loved us." The word *agape* is used in these verses and in all other verses that indicate or state that this love comes from God. So, in order for us to begin to see what God is revealing to us concerning love, let us use the word *gospelove* for the Greek word *agape*.

What do you think of when you hear or see the word "gospel"? Webster's dictionary defines "gospel" as the message concerning Christ, the kingdom of God, and salvation." Another part of that definition says, "an interpretation of the Christian message."

The word for gospel that is used in the New Testament is *euangelion* from the Greek. The word literally means "good news" and is usually translated as "gospel". Many of us are familiar with the Christmas story, and there we read, "But the angel said to them, 'Do not be afraid. I bring you good news that will cause great joy for all the people. Today in the town of David a Savior has been born to you; he is the Messiah, the Lord.'" (Luke 2:10-11) Whenever the word "gospel" is used, it always is referring to and contains within it the message of redemption. In John 3:16 we read, "For God so loved (gospeloved) the world that he gave his one and only Son, that whoever believes in him shall not perish but have eternal life." That is the essence of the "good news", the "gospel". What God is doing from Genesis to Revelation is all about redemption, as stated in Colossians 1:19-20, "For God was pleased to have all his fullness dwell in him (Christ), and through him to reconcile to himself all things, whether things on earth or things in heaven, by making peace through his blood, shed on the cross."

When the word *agape* is used, it comes from God and goes back to God. 1 John 4:7-10 reveals gospelove most clearly, "Dear friends, let us *gospelove* one another, for *gospelove* comes from God. Everyone who *gospeloves* has been born of God and knows God. Whoever does not *gospelove* does not know God, because God is *gospelove.* This is how God showed his *gospelove* among us. He sent his one and only Son into the world that we might live through him. This is *gospelove:* not that we *gospeloved* God, but that he *gospeloved* us and sent his Son as an atoning sacrifice for our sins." Now, we can contrast this *agape (gospelove)* with *fileo,* love as we know it. This is a strong, powerful love and is very much a part of all of our lives. The major difference with *agape* is that *fileo* begins with us and ends with us. Certainly, there will be some giving involved, but even that giving comes mostly from self-centered interests. Also, *fileo* involves some kind of attraction, affection, or desire and is not usually something we can will or decide. Thus, we fall in love (*fileo*), whereas with *agape, gospelove* is an act of the will, a choice of obedience to Christ. So, to contrast *fileo* with *agape* we will use the term *naturalove*. Certainly these terms seem awkward, perhaps even cumbersome, but until we can look at *agape* without reverting to our default concept of love (*fileo*), we will not have the definition and direction to experience and express God's *gospelove*.

In the gospel (redemptive good news) of Mark, Jesus asked, "Of all the commandments, which is the most important?" Jesus answers, "The most important one is this: 'Hear O Israel: The Lord our God, the Lord is one. *Gospelove* the Lord your God with all your heart and with all your soul and with all your mind and with all your strength. The second is this: *Gospelove* your neighbor as yourself. There is no commandment greater than these." (Mark 12:28-31) In the church and Christian literature, this is known as the Great Commandment, and rightly so. In most churches, you probably will find this verse or a version of it somewhere on a wall, plaque, or screen. "Love God and love your neighbor." We teach it, preach it, sing it, memorize it, wear it on tee shirts and wrist bands. I believe we are sincere and we really mean to carry out this commandment. In spite of all our efforts, though, we just do not express this kind of love. Why? Our default definition and understanding of love (*naturalove)* becomes the foundation for our love, so while we are reaching for *gospelove,* we are really trying to obey the command through *naturalove.*

In Luke 6:27-28, Jesus says, "But to you who are listening I say: Love (gospelove) your enemies, do good to those who hate you, bless those who curse you, pray for those who mistreat you." This is included in the command to "*gospelove* our neighbor". However, when we approach this directive from *naturalove,* obedience becomes impossible. We certainly have no affection, fondness, kinship, or desire to *naturalove* those who are our enemies, who hate us, who curse us, or mistreat us. In and of ourselves, we cannot *gospelove* these people. This *gospelove*, however, is commanded by Jesus. It is an act of the will and really has little or nothing to do with how we feel. That is a contrast we can see with naturalove and gospelove.

So, how do we do this? We are going to explore how we can move from the default concept of what we have always called love (*naturalove*) to know, receive, experience, and express *gospelove*. I am convinced that if those who follow Christ and those who come to follow Christ, can experience God's *gospelove* and show that *gospelove* to their world, we can truly be the salt and light to the world. GOD GOSPELOVES YOU!

CHAPTER ONE

OUT OF AFRICA, INTO AFRICA

    We were living and serving as missionaries in Durban, South Africa. It was in the 1980's and apartheid was still the rule of law in that African nation. There was strong anti-American sentiment as economic sanctions had been enforced, spearheaded by the American government. We were pastoring an English-speaking church in Durban and also working with the nearby Zulu Bible College as well as numerous churches of people of East Indian origin. The work was diverse and challenging, particularly as the message of Jesus, particularly *gospelove,* seemed often to be in direct contrast to the laws of the land. My wife, LaVonna, and our three children, Todd, Kevin, and Miriam were a vital part of this adventure. Communication with the United States was sporadic, at best, as these were pre-internet days and there was mostly a boycott of any American news in the country. Nevertheless, we were experiencing God's move in our lives and in the people with whom and to whom we were ministering.

    One night, I came home from a meeting of some kind and found that the family had already gone to bed. I wanted to unwind a bit, so I put a videotape into the VCR (remember those) that I had received from our mission headquarters in the United States. It was a video that helped us keep in touch with what was going on in the world and in our church around the world. I was not paying close attention, thinking about many things, when I suddenly became aware of what was on the video. It was a segment of news about our mission around the world. I heard the words that the Church of the Nazarene had registered in the country of Uganda and was preparing to enter that country. I do not know for certain how to describe it, but something took place in my mind and heart. I could not stop thinking about it. I went to bed and thought that I would probably forget about it the next morning. How wrong I was! I could not stop thinking about it all day long. As I prayed about it, I asked the Lord what I should do and it became apparent that I needed to share it with LaVonna.

LaVonna and I have been married a long time. We were married when she was eighteen, two weeks out of high school. When she married me (and of course I married her), I was in college and on a basketball and baseball scholarship. I really had no other ambition to do anything but play professional baseball. When I graduated from college and realized that professional baseball was not going to happen for me, I realized I needed some direction for our future. After a few months, God directed us toward ministry. While LaVonna was not totally against the idea, she did have her own anxieties. She grew up in the church and her image of a pastor's wife was someone who wore her hair piled on her head, wore long dresses and played the piano. None of that really fit LaVonna. However, even as a young woman, she was a spiritual lady and she recognized that God was leading. We accepted a call to a church in Nebraska and packed a U-Haul trailer with all of our belongings, and she and I and our four month old son, Todd, started our ministry adventure.

I look back on those days and realize I really had no sense of how much God loved me. I certainly had little knowledge and comprehension of *gospelove* and what that meant for me personally and for the ministry God had called me to. I had been raised in the church and attended a Christian college, but as I recall those days, I realize I was on the wrong track. We looked earlier at John 3:16, but I failed to realize the importance of John 3:17, "For God did not send his Son into the world to condemn the world, but to save the world through him." It seemed our emphasis in the church that I knew was condemnation first and maybe if we could persevere, someday we might understand and even experience that God could *gospelove* us. We were constantly looking at people through the lens of condemnation. Do they smoke, do they drink alcohol, do they dance, do they go to movies, etc.? So, most of our messages and teachings were on things we thought people should **not** be doing. Even though we had some great old hymns about God's great love, we mostly gave them a miss and focused on sin and condemnation rather than the *gospelove* of Jesus.

From our assignment in Nebraska, we moved to Kansas City to attend graduate seminary, then from there to a mission assignment to the Netherlands, where our second son, Kevin, was born, and then to pastor churches in Idaho and California before we received the call to South Africa. When we prayed and talked about each decision, I could often receive confirmation through LaVonna when she would express that she sensed that it was God's will to move in that particular direction. So, I knew that I needed to talk to her about what I was feeling about Uganda. Later that next day, before the kids came home from school, I gingerly approached her and shared with her what I sensed when I told her about the video and Uganda. After I spoke to her, there was a moment of silence until she finally said, "Gary, if you want to have your midlife crisis, go and do it by yourself. I am already in Africa and I don't need to go to Uganda." Wow! Well, I thought, that answers that and I put any thoughts of Uganda out of my mind.

Over the next two weeks, I tried not to think about the video and about Uganda, but it would just not let go of me. Then I realized that if the church put out that announcement, they probably already had a plan of sending someone there and beginning the work. I decided to

3

write to our regional director (no, not email or even a fax, but a snail mail letter) and tell him of my interest. I was sure he would reply with a "thanks, but no thanks response" and that they had someone they would send there. That would get me off the hook with God and my conscience would be clear, so I sent off the letter. I did not, however, say anything about it to LaVonna (big mistake). A week or so later, I received a letter from the regional office. Thinking it was my exoneration letter, I eagerly opened it and read it. To my great surprise, the regional director said that he was intrigued by my interest and that we should discuss it further. One part of me was interested and excited; another part was dreading going back to LaVonna and sharing what I had done.

When I told her about the letter and had her read it, she took the letter, wadded it up and threw it at me! We had a long way to go. Over the next few months, we met with the field director from East Africa and continued to seek God's will. If we went, it would mean that after a few months in the US, we would leave our oldest son there to begin college and our two youngest (we had added a lovely daughter, Miriam, to our family) would most likely have to attend a boarding school. This was certainly not something LaVonna had signed up for. Through several months of soul-searching times before God, we both came to the place where we believed this was God's will and direction for our lives. When I heard LaVonna say to me that if going to Uganda was God's will for our lives, then He also meant that boarding school was best for our children. That was again a final confirmation for me.

While our ministry in South Africa was fulfilling and an amazing period of spiritual growth for our whole family, the concept of God's *gospelove* was not in the forefront of my thinking and experience. The seeds were there, however, and God was faithful to continue to reveal Himself to me in ways I had never experienced. Before we

4

returned to the United States for a few months, I was speaking for a missionary retreat for all of our missionaries in Southern Africa. Our global director for world mission would be there and we would interview him for the final step in our assignment to East Africa. The morning after we met with him, I was preparing to speak for our final service together. The global director came in and he said that he had been talking with the regional director and they were excited about our new assignment and that the regional director would give me all of the details. The regional director came in and took me aside and told me that he got the final okay and we would proceed with the plans. Then, he said something quite surprising. He asked me if we would consider Rwanda as a part of the assignment. To be honest, even though I was in Africa, I had not heard of Rwanda. This was some years before the genocide took place and the only claim to fame for Rwanda was the mountain gorillas. Rwanda borders Uganda on the south and, during the colonial days was ruled by Belgium and was French speaking. We accepted the assignment, not knowing what was ahead, but over the years, it became apparent that God was in control. In fact, none of us were aware of what He was already doing in preparing the way. His *gospelove* was moving in us, people in the country and region as His wonderful redeeming, reconciling plan was being formed.

Civil war would come to Rwanda, but there was another war God describes in the book of Revelation. "Then war broke out in heaven." (Revelation 12:7) I had certainly read these words before, undoubtedly numerous times as I read through the book of Revelation. This time, though, they seemed to be more than just words. All kinds of thoughts and images began to go through my mind. For most of us, whatever we may think heaven is or is not, we certainly do not put war into the picture. Do we not think of heaven as peaceful, even serene? Heaven would be the one place where we would absolutely rule out war of any kind. After all, there is no crying there, right?

(Revelation 21:4) So how could there be war? Nevertheless, the words were there, and when I looked again, they were still there.

Then war broke out in heaven. Michael and his angels fought against the dragon and the dragon and his angels fought back. But he was not strong enough, and they lost their place in heaven (now, there's a scary thought). The great dragon was hurled down— that ancient serpent called the devil, or Satan, who leads the whole world astray. He was hurled to the earth, and his angels with him. (Revelation 12:7-9)

I realize that many of you may do what I did for a long time. Oh well, that's just Revelation, and I cannot really understand it and it certainly has little, if any, relevance to my daily life. However, as I thought about these words, I began to realize that perhaps they had something to say to me and my life. I eagerly went to various commentaries to see what the learned scholars had concluded about this passage. I was somewhat disappointed as I found surprisingly little information on what this war was really about. There were some references to perhaps the dragon being hurled to the earth was a pre-Genesis event, but most did not accept this and placed it in the drama that is to unfold at the end of the age. One of the difficulties in understanding much of the vision God gave to John is that we do live in time and space, and therefore, we are very linear. By linear, I mean that we like to put everything on a time line so we know what comes before and after.

When we look at Revelation, we have before, during, and after all seemingly happening at once. It is difficult to know how or where to place some of the things on the time line. So I am not sure when the war in heaven took place or is perhaps going to take place, but we can certainly see the effect of that war. We are not given much information on the cause of the war, but from the context of the Word of God, we can be fairly certain that it was some kind of rebellion led by the dragon, most likely Lucifer, an angel called the morning star. He evidently wanted a greater place in the kingdom of heaven and enlisted others to follow him. So he was hurled down to the earth along with his followers. We have questions about this that seem to have no answers, at least at the present time. Why was he sent to earth? Why was he given dominion over the kingdom of this world, as we learn from Luke 4:6, when Satan said to Jesus concerning the kingdoms of the world, "I will give you all their authority and splendor, for it has been given to me."

Though we may not understand why, we can begin to see a context for God's creation of man. In Genesis 1:26, we read, "Then God said, 'Let us make man in our image, in our likeness, and let them rule over the fish of the sea and the birds of the air, over the livestock, over all the earth, and over all the creatures that move along the ground.'" They were also told by God to be fruitful and multiply and continue to rule, or subdue, the earth. The broad stroke of the Word of God, from Genesis to Revelation, is not only God's interaction with man, but also God's covenant with man. This covenant was fueled by God and His gospelove. The placement of Adam and Eve in the Garden of Eden was God's covenant and activity to take back the earth from Satan. GOSPELOVE! Now, God being the infinite God, there are many ways He could accomplish this, but He has chosen to involve man and woman in His great plan.

The basic premise of God's covenant is "I will be your God, and you will be my people," and through this covenant, God will show the world who He is and what His purpose is. From the beginning, it is a redemptive covenant, "to reconcile to himself all things, whether things on earth or things in heaven" (Colossians 1:20). He has chosen to do this through gospelove. Romans 5:8 declares, "But God demonstrates his own love for us in this: While we were still sinners, Christ died for us." GOSPELOVE! A covenant is "a formal and serious agreement or promise between two parties." God is the initiating party, which is a great thing for us, for what could we possibly bring to the table that would be important enough for God. Interestingly, what He really asks of us throughout all of Scripture is obedience; He does all the rest. In John 14:15 Jesus says, "If you gospelove me, keep (obey) my commandments."

I do not know how long Adam and Eve lived in the fullness of this covenant. When we read the account in Genesis, it seems as if they no sooner got settled before they disobeyed God. When you think about it, though, time, as we know it may not have been introduced yet. God told Adam and Eve not to eat of the tree of the knowledge of good and evil or they would surely die. What do you think they understood of death, seeing as how they were created in the image of God? We know they disobeyed God, but did not immediately die. Time, then, became their enemy as it would ultimately lead them to death. What lead them to break the covenant with God and disobey Him? Genesis 3:4-5 says, "You will not surely die", the serpent said to the woman. "For God knows that when you eat of it your eyes will be opened, and you will be like God, knowing good and evil." It seems as if the same thread that led to the rebellion in heaven is the root of all sin: wanting to be like God. Most of us would immediately protest that we do not want to be like God. However, when we disobey what we know to be God's commands, we are saying that we want to make our own choices and assume control over our own destiny. We are not satisfied with being the obedient part of the covenant. We do not trust the all encompassing gospelove of Jesus Christ.

When we read through the remainder of Genesis 3, we see that the introduction of disobedience, or sin, changes everything. Adam and Eve's relationship to God was now different. They were cast out of the garden and their relationship to the environment was radically different. The intimacy of God's gospelove had been broken and the relationship was distant and estranged. Even though Adam and Eve had broken the covenant of this gospelove, God did not stop coming after them or stop initiating and continuing His covenant. That is the nature of gospelove. God did not give up on them, as gospelove never does as He helped clothe them and continued to communicate with them. His covenant was still in force; I will be your God and you will be my people. It is difficult even now for us to see the depth and breadth of God's grace and His gospelove. Certainly, He must have been disappointed by the actions of Adam and Eve. Would that not have been enough to invalidate the covenant? For any of us, it would certainly have brought it into question. If not there, then how about in Genesis 6:5-8, "The Lord saw how great man's wickedness on the earth had become, and that every inclination of the thoughts of his heart was only evil all the time. The Lord was grieved that he had made man on the earth, and his heart was filled with pain." God went on to say that He would wipe all mankind from earth, so great was His grief. But then, we come to verse 8, "But Noah found favor, or grace, in the eyes of the Lord." GOSPELOVE NEVER GIVES UP!

Think about that for a moment. There were by now quite a number of people on the earth. They were all wicked, so wicked that every inclination of their thoughts and of their hearts were only evil all the time. Wow! No wonder God's heart was filled with pain and He was grieved that He had ever made man. Surely, now would be the time to give up on the covenant. But God found one, Noah, to which He was willing to extend the grace of gospelove. The Bible says that Noah was a righteous man, blameless among the people of his time. You have to wonder, what with the widespread wickedness of the day, what a blameless man of his time looked like. Whatever it was, it was enough for God to give him grace and to save His creation of man through him. God's covenant was still in effect, although one could argue how effective it was in establishing the kingdom of God in this world.

Many of us know some of the story of Abraham and how God formed a nation through him that became God's own people. Their mission was to obey God and His commands and He would be their God, revealing His holiness, power, righteousness, and gospelove to the world, thus redeeming the world and reconciling it back to Him. As with all covenants, it came with a promise. His promise to the nation of Israel, the covenant people of Abraham, was that if they obeyed His commands all would go well with them. As you read through the Old Testament, God always kept His promise and His blessing, provision, and protection were consistently with the nation of Israel. It is interesting to see when things were not going well with them. It always seemed to begin with faulty, sloppy, or insincere worship. Their greatest sin against God was a divided loyalty, much like Lucifer, much like Eve, and much like us. There were numerous times in the history of Israel that it would seem as if God would give up the covenant. After all, they consistently broke the covenant by their disobedience to God. God was always faithful, always keeping His part of the covenant. It certainly looked as if His plan to use man in a covenantal relationship to redeem His creation was a monumental failure.

I suppose it would be natural for us to assume that God tried these covenants with Adam and Eve, Noah, Abraham and the people of Israel, and as each one failed, He decided to try something different. So now, He has to pull out the big gun and send His Son, Jesus. However, from God's perspective as revealed in His Word, His covenant has never changed nor has His purpose. He is reconciling all things unto Himself, things on the earth, and things in the heavens. Because we are living in time and space, that becomes our perspective of all things. However, God transcends time and space, so that these are not necessarily separate events, as they are with us; they are each a part of a whole. The whole is God's redemptive purpose in His creation. While we may have difficulty seeing the whole, we can certainly see God's plan will never work. He can never overcome Satan and the kingdom of this world through a covenant relationship with man. At least, from our perspective, that is the way it would seem to many, if not most of us.

Now, it is likely that most of us do not think in these terms. We leave that to the "professional" theologians, such as college and seminary professors or perhaps some pastors and missionaries. If we have grown up or spent time involved in a church, we have probably lived in and through a considerable amount of frustration. The frustration comes from never being good enough for God. We have broken too many rules or commandments and we just cannot live up to any standard that the church puts forward or that we perceive might be acceptable to God. If we have seldom or never been a part of a church, we perhaps think that "religion" is mostly about rules and regulations and that many if not most people who attend or take part are hypocrites.

When I started elementary school, I became aware that school was full of competition. I was the youngest of three children, as my brother was eight years older than me and my sister was five years older. Being that much younger, I guess I thought that I needed to somehow make my presence known or recognized and competition was one way to do that. I learned that if I tried hard enough, I could be successful in almost all of the endeavors associated with school. I could run faster, jump higher and farther, throw the ball harder and farther than any of the other kids my age. I was the school yo-yo champion by the fifth grade (aren't you impressed), but it was not only on the playground where I found competition. The classroom offered numerous ways to excel and be recognized, so I represented our school at the county spelling bee, where as a sixth grader, I competed against seventh and eighth graders from all of the schools in the county. I not only achieved the best grades on the report cards, but every test or project in every subject presented me with the challenge to be recognized as the highest scorer or best in class. I thought this would make my parents proud and give me some recognition along with my siblings. Ironically, I created a standard where the only direction I could go was down. I realized years later that I was living in a tyranny of success, so nothing was ever quite good enough. My father and mother expected me to be top of the class and it was only if I wasn't that they ever made any comment.

It took me longer than it should have to realize how this experience shaped my understanding or experience of a relationship with God the Father or with Jesus the Christ. I thought I needed to impress God with the way I tried to impress everyone else, from family to friends to coaches to teachers. As I went through my teenage years, I began to realize that I could not perform well enough for God. I sometimes felt as if I was constantly on a balance beam like gymnasts use in competition. I would go to church on Sunday and sort everything out as far as God was concerned, but most weeks I could barely make it to Tuesday before I fell off the balance beam of righteousness, disappointed God and started all over again. That became a seemingly never-ending cycle that I just could not break. After I began the ministry journey, I found that there was considerable competition even in that field. One could get recognition of the fastest growing church, most new members, most baptisms, most money raised, etc. I would work toward those areas to receive recognition from my colleagues and superiors, but

I did hope deep down that perhaps God might be impressed with my achievements. However, I was never quite sure and always felt that he was expecting more from me.

When I was about five years old, during a Sunday service at our church, the song leader, as we called them in those days, asked me to come forward to the platform and to sing a song. I do not remember if this was arranged beforehand or just spontaneous on his part, but I went up, stood on my tiptoes so I could reach the microphone they had and sang a song that we would often sing in Sunday School, "Jesus loves me, this I know, for the Bible tells me so." I am sure I believed that song as much as a five year old could as I sang it that day, but experiencing that gospelove would prove to be far more difficult than singing about it. I could teach and preach about the gospelove of God, but I did not seem to be able to really experience what I was preaching about.

Remember the railroad track with the two tracks that have to be completely in sync so that the train can move forward on its journey? We identified those tracks as *definition* and *direction*. We have distinguished between *agape* and *fileo* as both of those words are translated as *love* in the English translation of the New Testament, though they have different meaning and application in their contexts. So, we are using the terms *gospelove* (agape) and *naturalove* (fileo). Hopefully, we can begin to understand that God has an amazing, overwhelming, lavishing, unfailing, unconditional, unrelenting expression of *gospelove* when He not only tells us, but also demonstrates His own *gospelove* for us and in us. When we hear or see those words, "God loves you", our default mechanism takes us to *fileo* and we fail "to grasp how wide and long and high and deep is the *gospelove* of Christ, and to know this *gospelove* that surpasses knowledge—that you may be filled to the measure of all the fullness of God." (Ephesians 3:18-19) I could read those incredible words, but my mind was still stuck on a *naturalove* that revolved around me, my feelings, my circumstances, how I was treated by those around me. I knew deep down that I was not experiencing "a *gospelove* that surpasses knowledge" and that I was being "filled to the measure of all the fullness of God". My desire was to follow God's direction for our life and ministry. On the basis of *naturalove,* everything I read and studied lead me to believe that I could experience this *gospelove* even though what I was really doing was living, or trying to, in *naturalove. A gospelove* "that surpasses knowledge" was not something that was encouraged by the congregations I pastored nor by the denominational leaders that were leading the ship. After all, we do not want to be "out of control" do we?

GOING WITH THE WIND

As I said before, when the regional director told me Rwanda would be part of the assignment, I had never heard of the country. I soon learned that Rwanda sits in the very heart of the continent of Africa. It is a small country, about the size of our state of Maryland. It is the most densely populated country in Africa. The people come primarily from two tribes or ethnic groups, the Hutu and the Tutsi. The Hutu comprise 85 per cent of the population and the Tutsi almost 15 per cent. There are two national languages, Kinyarwanda and French. Everyone speaks Kinyarwanda and people who have had some kind of education can usually speak French. The country is very agrarian, and even though it is the land of a thousand hills, most of these hills have fertile volcanic soil and are used for growing food. While the crops can sustain the population, if there is any kind of hiccup in the rainy season, it can often lead to food shortages.

The main religions are animism and Christianity, with the largest segment of Christianity being Roman Catholic. In the last seventy-five years, though, there has been a growing evangelical presence developing. As we prepared for our assignment, I was somewhat surprised that no one sat down with me and said that this is our strategy when we enter a new country or this is what we expect to hopefully realize in the next five years. What I did not know is that at the same time that I was meeting with our global and regional directors, God was already putting things in motion according to His redemptive purpose. In John 3:5, Jesus says "Very truly I tell you, no one can enter the kingdom of God unless they are born of water and the Spirit. Flesh gives birth to flesh, but the Spirit gives birth to the spirit. You should not be surprised at my saying, 'You must be born again.' The wind blows wherever it pleases, you hear its sound, but you cannot tell where it comes from or where it is going. So it is with everyone born of the Spirit." This is a Scripture passage that we love to quote and refer to, but quite frankly, we hardly believe a word of it. To not know where something is coming from or where it is going is not a part of how we believe the church should develop in our world. We want to be in control and make sure everything is orthodox, within all of the guidelines of the particular polities, pieties, and principals that we have so carefully and painfully worked toward over centuries. We have more input as to how the church operates from management gurus in our world than from Jesus! More about that later.

What I did not know is that the wind of the Spirit was beginning to blow in ways that I could never have strategized. After we arrived in East Africa, we were staying in Nairobi, Kenya, which is where our field office was located. We were not registered in Rwanda, so we could not obtain visas to live there. We made a trip to Uganda to see about living there and working in both Uganda and Rwanda, but we could not sense God's clear direction for that and He seemed to be leading to Rwanda.

I made an exploratory trip to see if I could get a sense of the lay of the land. I was struck by the beauty of this tiny country as the hills were picturesque as crops would be terraced all the way to the top. The people were friendly and open, and I found some great help within the missionary community. Other denominations and organizations welcomed me and our church with open arms, refreshingly portraying a kingdom-of-God perspective, saying we need all of the help we can get. As I flew back to Kenya, I began to ask God how we should go about beginning the work. Little did I know that the wind of the Holy Spirit was blowing and He was going to show me.

When I returned to Nairobi, there was a letter waiting for me from our denominational headquarters in Kansas City. When I opened it, I found a letter that had been forwarded to me from Rwanda. As I read it, I was truly astounded. It was from Rev. Andre Samvura and he said that he was a pastor in the Eglise du Nazareen au Rwanda (Church of the Nazarene in Rwanda). He said they had several churches, and if there was a missionary anywhere close to Rwanda, could they come and visit and perhaps help them. Making contact was not easy and it took me two trips from Kenya to Rwanda to locate them and schedule a meeting. Andre had arranged a meeting in the town of Gisenyi, which was on the Rwanda/Congo border. I was so excited to meet the group and see what they were all about. When I arrived at the meeting, there was another group and I quickly learned that they were from across the border in Zaire (which was what Congo was called at the time). They proudly told me they were from the Eglise du Nazareen au Zaire (Church of the Nazarene in Zaire). I was amazed as there were perhaps twenty pastors there from the two countries. So I asked, how did this happen? How and why did you begin the Church of the Nazarene?

There was a Bible College in Goma, Zaire, at the time. Gisenyi, Rwanda, and Goma, now Congo, are twin cities divided by the border of the two countries. They are both sitting on the edge of Lake Kivu. The Bible College was non-denominational and two of the students were Andre Samvura from Gisenyi and Tombo Wilondja from Goma. Both young men were called to ministry and were trying to decide in what church or organization they were going to minister.

One day in class, an American missionary who was teaching mentioned the Church of the Nazarene in the course of his lecture. I do not know for sure what he said or what description he gave, but it piqued the interest of Tombo. He tried to find out more about the church, but was not able to find much information. One of his friends and fellow students was going to Amsterdam, the Netherlands for a major evangelical worldwide conference. Tombo asked him if he found someone from the Church of the Nazarene, could he ask him for some information that he could give to Tombo. The student from Congo soon met a district superintendent from Haiti. They both spoke French, so they talked together. The student explained that he had a friend, Tombo, who wanted to know about his church. The man from Haiti gave his address and said to have Tombo write to him. When the student from Congo returned to Goma, he told Tombo about the man from Haiti and gave Tombo the address.

Tombo wrote to Haiti and explained who he was and what he wanted. The superintendent returned his correspondence and sent Tombo a Manual of the Church of the Nazarene printed in French and authorized Tombo to begin the Church of the Nazarene in Congo. I saw that letter of authorization and thought about the wind of the spirit, as I knew that if that Superintendent had gone through "proper" channels, the story would have taken quite a different direction, much more predictable. Tombo took that Manual and that letter and started the church in Goma and surrounding areas in Congo.

This was the same time that God was calling us from South Africa to what we thought was Uganda, but God had Rwanda and Congo in His plan and direction. Shortly thereafter, Andre Samvura from Rwanda talked with Pastor Tombo and learned that he had begun the church. He began to help Pastor Tombo and read through the Manual. He then found a copy machine of some kind, copied the pages of the Manual, and began the Church of the Nazarene in Rwanda. We had started for Uganda, but the wind of the Spirit turned us toward Rwanda and Congo, not knowing what God had already begun. That is often the way of the Holy Spirit, "The wind blows wherever it pleases. You hear its sound, but you cannot tell where it comes from or where it is going." When Jesus says in John

3:6 "Flesh gives birth to flesh, but the Spirit gives birth to spirit", He is also talking about *gospelove* and *naturalove*. *Gospelove* is of the Spirit and is lavished on us and in us as we are "born of the Spirit". This is God's redemptive love and His redemptive wind, blowing in His direction to reconcile all of creation unto Himself. He desires to make a new creation.

WHAT'S NEW?

"Therefore, if anyone is in Christ, he is a new creation; the old is gone, the new is come." (2 Corinthians 5:17)

Have you ever been to any of your high school reunions? I remember being able to attend the fifteen year reunion of our class. I had not seen most of my classmates since graduation, so I was anxious to see some friends from high school and some of my teammates from the athletic teams I had been a part of. I was also interested to see the reaction of many of them when I told them I was a pastor, as that is not exactly the direction in which I was headed when they knew me. As we entered, we were given a name badge, which displayed a picture from our senior year that was in our yearbook. I chuckled when I saw my picture, quite sure that I still looked exactly that (except for 20 extra pounds, a mustache, longer hair, and a few wrinkles) and no one would have trouble recognizing me. As the evening went on, however, I was grateful for those photos as I was surprised how much everyone else (not me, though) had changed in the past fifteen years. I remember one classmate in particular. When I saw her, I was aware that she recognized me and called me by name. I had no idea who she was and thought she must be a spouse of one of my classmates. When I finally maneuvered myself, unobtrusively, of course, so I could see her name tag, I was in shock. I tried to keep my composure, but I am sure she caught the surprise and astonishment in my reaction. As I saw her picture and read her name, memories came flooding back to my mind. She was, to be kind about it, the proverbial *nerd* in our high school days. She was brilliant, one of the top students in our class. She was definitely socially awkward, as she seemed to give little attention to her appearance She was a bit overweight, her hair was usually somewhat long and stringy, her complexion far from smooth. She wore thick glasses, unfashionable clothes with high knee socks that no other girl in our class would wear. She was nice, somewhat shy. I do not know for sure, but I doubt she had many, if any dates in high school. As I blinked to cover my shock and focus on the young woman standing before me, I was still having trouble reconciling her with the name tag. Perhaps she switched with the real named person as a joke. She was no longer overweight, but perfect and shapely in every way. Her hair was short and very stylish. Her complexion was flawless and the thick eyeglasses were gone as I suppose she was wearing contact lenses. There was still a bit of shyness, but as we talked, there was also a confidence that was apparent as she talked. As I thought about her later, I realized that my surprised reaction was probably something she was looking forward to and I doubt I was the only one who reacted that way.

As I reflected more on my classmate, I more than once considered her as a completely different person. She certainly was on the outside. I did not know her well in high school and I only briefly talked to her at the reunion, but I really do not know if she was a different person or not. Some time ago I had lunch with another high school classmate. He and I had been close friends through school and had connected a few times since then, though not quite often. Now, we are a lot more than fifteen years down the road, but as we reminisced together, he made a statement that I had not changed much, that I was basically the same person he knew in school. I thought to myself how wrong he was. Maybe my voice sounded the same (I am now more honest to know I do not look like I did in high school), and as we talked about mutual friends and some of our experiences together, he just assumed I was the same person. In reality, I was nothing like I was in high school. Yes, age, experience, and time changes you, but I am completely different. You see, I am a new *creation* in Christ Jesus.

I would be interested in knowing how many of you reading this would consider yourself a new creation in Christ. There are perhaps many of you that would consider yourself a Christian. Depending on your background, you perhaps have had some experience of becoming a Christian. You may label it in various ways; being saved, being born again, accepting Christ as Savior, trusting in Christ, becoming a believer, being baptized. So, could I ask you something? From the time you had this experience until now, what has taken place in your life? Are you different? Has the old gone, as the verse in 2 Corinthians 5:17 says? Has the new come? Would you consider yourself a new creation in Christ? Would you describe your life as being a follower of Jesus Christ in your daily life? In your marriage? At your job? How do you spend your money? How do you spend your time? What kind of friends do you have? How do you treat your body? Some of you may think that this guy sure is nosy. What does all of this have to do with being a Christian?

My purpose is certainly not to minimize any experience we may have had with God through Christ. I would like to draw our attention to God's purpose, which we saw was and is to reconcile all things on earth and in the heavens to God through what Christ has done, making peace through the shedding of his blood. Again, we may ask, "What does this have to do with me and my marriage, my job, my money, my friends, my body? I believe the Jesus *gospelove* answer is: Everything! What I have found through many years of ministry is that there is a significant gap between our experience of "becoming a Christian" and the reality of being a follower of Jesus, a new creation in Christ. We have relegated the purpose of the kingdom of God versus the kingdom of this world to the "called" ones. You know, the pastors, evangelists, and missionaries.

We have little idea or concept of how our ordinary lives can fulfill the purposes of God in establishing his kingdom through His covenant with us. In fact, most of us who call ourselves Christians are not too concerned with the kingdom of God's purpose and how it is to be fulfilled. We have accepted a gospel that is primarily concerned with the forgiveness of our sins and how do we get to heaven when we die? How did this happen? How did we get seemingly off track? Remember the train track and the two tracks that have to be in sync and traveling in the same direction? The reality is that we started in the wrong direction! For about a hundred years, since the early part of the twentieth century, the church of Jesus Christ in America has presented what I would call "gospelight" rather than "gospelove". We have not really come to terms with "gospelove", so our definition is faulty, incomplete to say the least. Then we started in the wrong direction, as we will explain. We are all familiar with the term "light" as it refers to something that is not heavy, or maybe even not complete. In other words, when we describe some product as "light" we understand the reference and usage. We know Pepsi light, light beer, light salad dressing, light ice cream, etc. For a product to contain the term "light", it means that there are some things not included that would be in the regular version. It may be fewer calories, less carbs, less fat, less sugar, but it is less something that can give the designation "light". In my opinion, it always means less taste. We now use the term for other things besides food products. Believe it or not, I have seen a few churches advertise one of their services as "church light". Interesting.

So, what do I mean by "gospel light" and why is that the track in the wrong *direction*? It began sincerely, with passion and zeal for Jesus and His church. We (when I say we, I include myself in the leaders of the church) wanted as many as possible to know the good news of the gospel of Jesus. The first half of the twentieth century was a season of mass evangelism. Gifted and passionate evangelists would hold large crusades where hundreds and sometimes thousands of people would attend. An invitation to accept Christ or any of the other labels we mentioned would be given and usually large numbers of people would respond. Much of the time, these crusades were not connected to any particular church, though the people who responded were encouraged to start attending a church. It was not long before many of the churches began to follow the same evangelistic pattern. Now, I believe God greatly used these evangelists, but we did not realize that to target such a great audience, we had to narrow the message to be short and direct.

So what became the popular and accepted message was primarily about sin and hell. The desired outcome became the possibility that one could be forgiven of their sins and could then receive eternal life in heaven and not in hell. That is biblically correct, of course, and it is an amazing gospel. However, what we have not realized is that giving only part of the gospel has led us to shape the message to the interest of man. "Gospel light" became the entry into a club, much like Costco or Sam's Club. You had to have a card to enter, which for us was the fact that I had said to someone, somewhere, the sinner's prayer and now my name was written on the membership list (the Lamb"s book of life). And we developed doctrines around this so that we basically would be members for eternity, whether we paid the membership dues or not. What was not so recognizable is that we became spiritual consumers, like members of Costco or Sam's. We would enter the church whenever it was convenient and say to the manager (presumably God, but sometimes the assistant manager, pastor, or priest) that we needed things—things like health, wealth, and happiness, new jobs, etc. Sometimes, we would earnestly ask for help in our marriage or raising our kids, but rarely did we think that we were in a *gospelove* covenant relationship.

Think about our way of contacting the manager. We call this prayer. If we are honest, most of us use prayer as a means to get something from God. God, please do this, provide that, bless this, fix that; we are constantly asking Him for things. Now, we are told in the Bible to ask, but there is a context for this communication. It is that through Christ Jesus, we are in a *gospelove* covenant relationship with the almighty God. The same basic covenant He established with Adam and Eve and the nation of Israel is the same one He still provides the people of His body, the church; I will be your God and you will be my people. So let me ask you, when you pray, does it sound like you are in a relationship? The reality is, we have not gotten on this track yet, the *gospelove* track, as we have started at the wrong end and are going in the wrong direction.

So, what do we mean when we say we started at the wrong end and got on the track going in the wrong direction. To help us, let us look at some Bible verses that are familiar with most everyone. Well, at least one of the verses is.

John 3:16-17

For God so loved (gospeloved) the world that he gave his one and only Son, that whoever believes in him shall not perish but have eternal life. For God did not send His Son into the world to condemn the world, but to save the world through him.

Many of us could quote or at least paraphrase verse 16, as it is one of the mostly widely known verses in all of the Bible. However, verse 17 is not nearly as well known and is usually ignored when it comes to this passage. How ironic, even tragic, it is, then, that many, probably most of us have come to Christ on the basis of verse 17. Those who have rejected Christ, or not given Him and his message and call to us much consideration, have also done so on the basis of verse 17.

While mass evangelism remained an often used and popular way to present the gospel of Jesus Christ, in the second half of the twentieth century we began to utilize what I would call "confrontational" evangelism or more popularly called "personal" evangelism. There were methods that became well known and often used across the country, such as the Roman Road to Salvation, Evangelism Explosion, and the Four Spiritual Laws. The "confrontational" aspect was that we were encouraged to present these methods to any one we came in contact with, whether we knew them or not. I remember going to conferences to learn these methods and how we could implement these in our local church. The presenter, who was usually a pastor of a large church or an evangelist of some renown, would share his own experience, most often of someone sitting next to him on an airplane, a "captive" audience. I marveled as I listened to how he entered the conversation and how often it seemed, at least from his telling, that the other person prayed to receive Christ before they landed at their destination. So, I thought I might have an opportunity as I had flown to the conference and perhaps I would have a "captive" audience on the flight home. I boarded the flight, secured my aisle seat and waited for my unsuspecting prospect to take their seat. Well, it did not seem to happen according to the script. No one sat in the middle seat and finally a man rather perfunctorily asked me to move so he could take his window seat. Everything about him radiated the vibe that he did not want to talk to anybody and he certainly did not want anyone to talk to him. Even the flight attendant had difficulty getting him to respond to her offerings of something to drink. I did try to engage in conversation a couple of times and was quickly, if not rudely rebuffed. After we landed, I was discouraged, perhaps even feeling guilty that I did not "lead someone to the Lord" that I was not certain I wanted to implement these methods in our congregation.

Again, I do not want to minimize these efforts at personal evangelism. It was a major attempt to move ministry out of the four walls of the church building and into areas of everyday life. Through the years, we found that though many made commitments to pray the sinner's prayer and receive Jesus as Savior, their connection to the church and continuing development of becoming a disciple of Jesus was a low percentage. Most of these "confrontational" evangelistic methods began with condemnation (John 3:17) and gradually, in most cases, tried to move to *gospelove.* As I mentioned before, I grew up in the church as my parents were committed and involved members of the church. Attending church was something we did every Sunday morning, Sunday night, and Wednesday night. As I recall those days, my perception was that we started with condemnation. In fact, we were so strong on the condemnation part that I cannot really recall much at all being taught or preached about *gospelove.* We sang about it in our hymns and learned some of the Scriptures, but it seemed church was all about the evils of smoking, drinking alcohol, movies, dances, and anything that referred to sex. Now, that is my perception and I am sure it was probably not that one sided. Actually, I am sure it was that one sided. During my teen years in the church, if we wanted to know if someone was a Christian, we had a litmus test question, "Does he smoke, drink, or chew, or go with girls that do?" You think I'm kidding, don't you?

My Dad was a wonderful churchman. He was always involved, made himself available, and served on the church board, was Sunday School Superintendent, Sunday School teacher, Missionary president, sang in the choir (not all of these at the same time). When we moved to a new town, I remember that there were two churches of our denomination in the town. One of them was considerably larger than the other, but my Dad chose the smaller one as he knew they needed help and that our family could be of help. At one point, after I had begun our ministry journey, Dad took the training his church was offering for one of these "confrontational" evangelistic methods. He went through all of the training and even helped lead someone to pray to receive Christ in their home. When He told me about it, I asked if he was excited by the possibility of reaching others for Christ through this method. He was brutally honest when he replied, "No, I will probably never use it." I asked him why not and he said that it was just not natural or relational. Now, through the years I watched my parents reach out in *gospelove* to several families that became believers and members of the church. It was not a program, method, or particular outreach emphasis, but the transforming *gospelove* of Jesus that reached out to touch others. My wife's parents were the same way, totally involved in the church, but their greatest impact through the years was the *gospelove* of Jesus as they shared Him with those around them. Ironically, what they were doing was not really recognized as ministry.

Ministry is what you did "at the church". I recall a Sunday morning when I was about 13 and the pastor gave an altar call for people to come to the altar and repent of their sins and receive Jesus as their Savior. Nothing wrong with that. I do not remember how many responded, but I do remember one man, though, because we had been in their home and my parents had befriended the couple. She was a believer in Jesus and came to church regularly, but her husband rarely came, only when their daughter was in some kind of church program. Here he was, though, not only in church, but now at the altar. My Dad and several other men in the church, including the pastor, were gathered around him, praying for him and with him. As I remember, he wept his way through repentance and seemed truly sincere to receive Jesus as Savior. I knew, though, that there was some kind of reckoning coming, because having been in their home, I knew that this man was a heavy smoker. And in those days, smoking was perhaps the most evil thing one could do. I know for certain that I heard more sermons on the evils of smoking than I did on the *gospelove* of Jesus. Sure enough, before this man could get to his car, the pastor confronted him about the fact that now that he was a Christian, he had to give up smoking, right now, this minute.

Whatever we may think of smoking, what if that pastor had told him how much Jesus *gospeloved* him and how much Jesus would be with him as he surrendered his life every day. I don't know for sure how that might have worked, but I do know that he never came to church again as long as we lived there.

I do not know where you may be in your spiritual journey, but what I do know is that Jesus *gospeloves* you. He died for you and for your sins. Have you been "born again"? When Jesus used this phrase, it was in a conversation he was having with a very religious man by the name of Nicodemus. (John 3:1-21) Nicodemus was a religious leader in that day, but Jesus had brought more than just religion, rituals, and rules. He had brought life, and that life was expressed through the *gospelove* of Jesus. So, when Jesus uses this term, born again, it also means born from above, or born of the (Holy) Spirit. John writes in his letter, "Everyone who loves has been born of God and knows God. Jesus starts in his conversation with Nicodemus with the *gospelove* of God. He could have easily started with the condemnation because the Pharisees, the religious leaders at that time, had much about them that could be condemned. So, Jesus does not mention here forgiveness of sins or hell (which does not mean they are not real or important), but He says that this birth, this birth of the *gospelove* of God is the only way to enter the kingdom of God. As we have seen in John 3:16-17, Jesus came not only to save us, but also to save the world through Him. Our salvation, being born of His *gospelove* and made a new creation is part of God's plan and purpose to save the world and establish His kingdom. How is He going to accomplish this? In the same way He has used since the beginning—through His covenant relationship with His people.

God is infinite. Do you believe that? There are many people in our world who say they believe in God, but then they try to define

God in their own terms. For instance, I have had numerous people say something like, "I can't believe in a God who. . .? You can fill in the rest. We do not define God. He is Who He says He is and we come to Him on His terms. We cannot really grasp all of what it means for God to be infinite, but we can believe it. That means that God can use infinite ways, situations, and circumstances to reconcile the creation to Himself.

Not too long after we were in Congo, I had a report back from Pastor Tombo, a report that was verified to me from other people who were there. He had gone to an area in Eastern Congo that was very rural and where there was a cluster of villages not far from each other. Pastor Tombo had taken several young "evangelists" with him. These "evangelists" were actually pastors in training, learning on the job. They went through these villages and told as many people as they could that they were going to have a meeting at the common soccer field that these villages used. The day and time came for the meeting and several hundred people from these villages came to hear Pastor Tombo tell them about Jesus. Just as he started to speak, it began to rain. When it rained in that area, it usually rained hard, which meant that the people would leave as there was no convenient shelter. Before they began to disperse, Pastor Tombo said in a loud voice, "Don't leave. We know a God who can stop the rain and we are going to call on Him to do it." He turned to his "evangelists" and asked them to pray that God would stop the rain. He raised his eyes to the heavens and began to call on God to stop the rain. The people stayed where they were, waiting to see what would happen. Within minutes, the rain began to let up, then it stopped completely. The clouds broke apart and the sun began to shine. The people thought that the pastor knew a God who could stop the rain, so they wanted to hear about Him.

At the end of his message, Pastor Tombo invited all who wanted to know this God to come forward and he would pray with them. Over two hundred people responded and we planted three churches in those villages from that one meeting. Nothing can stop the reconciling wind of the Holy Spirit.

Do you believe that God really stopped the rain and parted the clouds in those villages in Congo? Of course, you don't. You are most likely an enlightened, reasonable, thoughtful American, and well, even if you do believe in God, that is just a little far out there. Most of you probably would say that the rain just happened to stop at that moment, which was good timing by Pastor Tombo, but there was no miracle of God stopping the rain. We had just been back from Africa for a short while and I was pastoring a church in Oregon. We had a pastor's conference that summer with all of the pastors from our denomination in the Northwest meeting at one of our college campuses. One afternoon we had some free time and it was unusually hot, so many of us took advantage of their Olympic sized pool. As I was in the water, I had a conversation with another pastor. He introduced himself and told me that he was pastor of a church in Colorado. I had spoken at a Missions conference in Colorado a few months before, so I asked him if he was there. He said that yes he was so I told him I was the missionary guest speaker. I looked a little different in the water in the swimming pool than on the platform in a church, but then he recognized me and said, "Oh, you were the one from Africa, right?" I said, "Yes, that's right". He went on to say that he and some members of his church enjoyed the stories I told from Africa and they talked about them on the ride home. Then, he said, "Of course, we did not believe any of them". Wow! I was speechless for a few moments and then he swam off to be with some of his friends.

So, how big is your God? That is an important question because the *gospelove* of Jesus comes to us from an infinite God. It is not a love that we can define, measure, limit, or fit to our definition. We read in Ephesians 3:17-19, "And I pray that you, being rooted and established in love, may have power, together with all the Lord's holy people, to grasp how wide and long and high and deep is the love of Christ, and to know this love that surpasses knowledge— that you may be filled to the measure of all the fullness of Christ." The love that is used here is agape, *gospelove*. We have already discovered that this is not something that is natural and that we can just decide to experience it. Rather, it comes from God and flows back to God, joining with His overarching, redemptive purpose of reconciling all things on earth (including you and me) and the heavens unto Himself.

Well, let us continue the conversation that Jesus has in John 3 with Nicodemus and try and continue to comprehend what the Word of God means that through Christ we can become "a new creation".

Perhaps it would help us at this point to use another label for becoming "a new creation": the word "saved". As I grew up in the church, the question most often asked of someone would be, "Are you saved?" I have to admit that for a long time, way too long, I did not connect being "saved" with God's *gospelove*. We need to remember the context that without the *gospelove* of Jesus, there would not be "a new creation in Christ" or being "born again or born from above" without being "born from the *gospelove* of God. Taken out of any context, the term "saved" could have all kinds of meanings. This is a good biblical word, perhaps first used in the context of our salvation by the angel who visited Joseph and told him that he should not be afraid to take Mary as his wife, because the child she was carrying was from the Holy Spirit. Then the angel said, "She will give birth to a son, and you are to give him the name

Jesus, because He will save His people from their sins" (Matthew 1:21). The angel was talking of Jesus as the Messiah, the anointed one who would bring deliverance to God's covenant people, Israel, and ultimately to all men. Let's begin to wean ourselves from the "gospel light" and move into the fullness of the *gospelove* of Jesus. Using the word "saved" as a label for becoming a new creation, let us consider what we are saved from, how we are saved, and what we are saved for or to.

What we are saved from. The angel said to Joseph that this child was coming to save people from their sins. When we look through the lens of "gospel light", we think of Jesus forgiving us of what we have done wrong so we will not go to hell. While all of that is true, we must look through the lens of *gospelove* so that we can start with the correct definition and start at the beginning going in the right direction. Adam and Eve had consequences when they disobeyed God and ate of the tree of the knowledge of good and evil. Their relationship with God was different, as was their relationship with each other, with the fields, and with the animals. They were barred from the garden. There was a separation between them and God that had not been there before. The consequences of that sin is expressed by Paul in Romans 5:12, "Therefore, just as sin entered the world through one man, and death through sin, and in this way death came to all men, because all sinned." He said earlier in Romans 3:23, "For all have sinned and fallen short of the glory of God." Then He says in Romans 6:23, "For the wages of sin is death." Most of us have a difficult time coming to terms with the hopelessness of our own situation. Okay, what can we do to make up for this sin or to show that we are really repentant? Just show me and I will do it. The reality is, though, that there is nothing we can do to make up for what we have done. We just do not want to accept that. We think this because we have little concept of the holiness and righteousness of God. Thankfully, God knows this and took matters in His own hand. He expressed and displayed His amazing *gospelove.*

Romans 5:6 says, "You see, at just the right time, when we were still powerless, Christ died for the ungodly." Verse 10 goes on to say, "For if, when we were God's enemies, we were reconciled to him through the death of his Son, how much more, having been reconciled, shall we be *saved* through his life." I love "how much more", don't you? John writes in 1 John 1:9. "If we confess our sins, he is faithful and just and will forgive our sins and purify us from all unrighteousness." *Gospelove* in action. "Gospel light", fueled by *naturalove*, focuses on the forgiveness of sins and our qualification for eternal life. The "how much more" is given as a promise in this verse. We are not only forgiven and pardoned for the sins we have committed, but we are cleansed and purified from the disease of sin we inherited from Adam. 1 John 3:8 states, "The reason the Son of God appeared was to destroy the devil's work." When we read that, does it bring to mind the love of God? No, probably not. Our definition, remember, must begin with the *gospelove* of Christ. Without the cleansing and purifying of the sin nature, we are still a slave to sin and we will find ourselves in much the same position as the nation of Israel. Even though they had the law and they had worship rituals where they would offer sacrifices for their sins and sometimes receive forgiveness through the prophet or priest, they were still powerless to keep the law or be obedient to God's command.

This "how much more" is explained further in Roman 8:3-4, "For what the law was powerless to do in that it was weakened by the sinful nature, God did by sending his own Son in the likeness of sinful man to be a sin offering. And so he condemned sin in sinful man, in order that the righteous requirements of the law might be fully met in us, who do not live according to sinful nature but according to the Spirit." Through what Jesus did on the cross *(gospelove),* we no longer have to be slaves to sin. We now are enabled and empowered through the Holy Spirit of Jesus living in us to live in obedience to God. Jesus broke the power of sin and the domination sin had over us. When we are born into the kingdom of God, we are no longer dominated by the values and directions of the kingdom of this world, which is under the control of Satan. We are saved from that domination. As John tells us in 1 John 1:7, "But if we walk in the light, as he (Jesus) is in the light, we have fellowship with one another, and the blood of Jesus, his Son, purifies us from all sin."

One of my favorite people we come to know in the Bible is David, the king of Israel. David was brave and courageous, killing animals when his life was threatened, taking down Goliath, and leading the army of Israel to numerous victories.

David was also a worshipper and led the nation in worshipping the Lord as he wrote songs and choruses for the nation to sing. David was also betrayed by his own sinful nature, as he so tragically demonstrated in his relationship with Bathsheba (read 2 Samuel 11-12). He committed adultery, lied about it, and finally was guilty of causing the death of the husband of Bathsheba, Uriah. In Psalm 51, David lets us in on his spiritual journey through that difficult time. David realized that there was a greater need he had than just forgiveness for his sins, though he certainly needed that. In verse 5 of Psalm 51, David says, "Surely I was sinful at birth, sinful from the time my mother conceived me." David became very aware he had a heart condition of sin.

In light of this revelation, he cries out in verse 10, "Create in me a pure heart, O God, and renew a steadfast spirit within me." David knew that he needed radical cleansing and purification of the heart in order to live in obedience to the Lord. When our daughter, Miriam, was a child, she would from time to time have problems with her ears. These problems would manifest in the form of earaches. We would give her children's aspirin or Tylenol to help relieve the pain. Thankfully, she would usually have some relief from the pain, but we would need to repeat the process every few hours. I knew, though, that while we were treating the symptoms, we were doing nothing about the real problem. You see, each time she had earaches, it was a signal that she had an ear infection. We would then take her to the doctor, who would diagnose the ear infection and prescribe antibiotics to fight the infection. After a couple of days, the antibiotic would effectively clear the infection and there would be no more earaches.

That is not unlike what God has done for us. The sins that we commit (according to Scripture, we have all committed sin) are the symptoms of an infectious condition, known as the sinful nature. The *gospelove* of Jesus has come to not only forgive us of our sins, but to cleanse and purify the disease of sin that we inherited. We are reminded again of the *gospelove* of Jesus as expressed in 1 John 1:9, "If we confess our sins (the symptoms), he (Jesus the Christ) is faithful and just and will forgive us our sins and purify as from all unrighteousness (take away the infection or disease of sin)." God has saved us from sin, its consequences, and its domination.

How are we saved? Let us look again at the big picture. God is in the process of reconciling all things on the earth and in the heavens unto Himself through what Christ did by making peace through his blood shed on the cross. God is establishing the kingdom of God in the kingdom of this world through His people, the reconciled ones. This purpose of God begins with *gospelove,* "For God so *gospeloved* the world that He sent His One and only Son to save the world" (John 3:16) Remember the conversation Jesus had with Nicodemus as recorded in John chapter 3? He quotes Jesus as telling us that the Holy Spirit is like the wind, and then He says, "The wind blows wherever it pleases. You hear its sound, but you cannot tell where it comes from or where it is going. So it is with everyone born of the Spirit" (John 3:8). The wind of the Holy Spirit that is blowing across the earth is a reconciling wind. As new creations in Christ, we are part of that wind as indicated by this verse. According to the Bible, we are so hopelessly lost in our sin that we cannot even begin to turn to God in our own strength.

So God blows the wind of the Spirit through our lives and testimonies. A wind of any strength gets our attention, doesn't it? We see its effect even though we do not see the wind itself. This is the way of God's grace. In theological terms, we call this prevenient grace. "Prevenient" is an interesting word. The dictionary defines "prevenient" as an adjective that means antecedent or anticipatory. God's prevenient grace goes before us as the reconciling wind of His Spirit blows across the kingdom of this world. Without that wind, we would not even know of our hopeless situation, but once the wind of God's grace gets our attention, we know that we are sinners, citizens of the kingdom of this world. We are powerless to do anything about it until the force of the wind of God's grace enables us to turn from our sin to God's reconciling provision.

GOSPELOVE!

This wind of God's grace is initiated by God. Romans 5:6 says, "You see, at just the right time, when we were still *powerless*, Christ died for ungodly." Why did he do this? *Gospelove,* as stated in Romans 5:8, "But God demonstrates his own love for us in this: While we were still sinners, Christ died for us." In fact, the Word declares that we were enemies of God and it was while we were enemies that Christ died for us. Just think about that for a moment. Do you have any enemies? If you do, what do you want to happen to them? Probably not what Jesus says in Luke 6:27-28, "Love (gospelove) your enemies, do good to those who hate you, bless those who curse you, pray for those who mistreat you." I doubt if you want to show them how much you love (naturalove) them. The death of Jesus on the cross is truly amazing grace, this wind of the Spirit that originates in the heart of God as *gospelove.* Perhaps an even more amazing thought is that as new creations in Christ, we become a part of this wind that God blows to the godless. Once we become aware of this wind of grace, what are we to do about it?

Paul writes to the Ephesian church about this grace in chapter 2, verses 8 and 9, "For it is by grace you have been saved, through faith—and this is not from yourselves, it is the gift of God— not by works, so that no one can boast." How does this grace work to save us? Through the wind of God's reconciling purpose, we become aware of our own condition of sin. Remember Jesus saying the wind was like the Spirit? When Jesus was telling His disciples that He was leaving, but He was sending the Holy Spirit to them, He told them how this wind of grace would blow in John 16:8, "When he (the Holy Spirit) comes, he will convict the world of guilt in regard to sin and righteousness and judgment." When the wind is strong enough, we become convinced of our own sin and of the righteousness of God and that we need to do something about it. Actually, it is God who has done something about it through sending His Son to die in our place for our sin. *Gospelove!* So what we really do is believe that God really did what He says He did.

In Acts chapter 2, we read of the wind of the Spirit blowing strongly in verse 2, "Suddenly a sound like the blowing of a violent wind came from heaven and filled the whole house where they were sitting." God then uses a new creation in Christ, Peter, as the voice of that wind, and as he preaches to a crowd, they become aware of their sin and God's righteousness. They did not know what to do from there, so they asked Peter what they should do. Peter replies in verse 38, "Repent and be baptized, every one of you, in the name of Jesus Christ for the forgiveness of your sins. And you will receive the gift of the Holy Spirit." He was describing what Jesus had said to Nicodemus, that the way to enter the kingdom of God is to be born of the Spirit. Let's take a closer look at Peter's response.

"Repent" is not a word that we regularly use today. In the New Testament, "repent" means a change of mind or a change of direction. There is also the sense of being sorry for the results of the previous direction. As used in the New Testament, there is certainly a moral sense to the word. Let us look again at 1 John 1:9, "If we confess your sins, he is faithful and just and will forgive us our sins and purify us from all unrighteousness." In our daily vernacular, there is a difference between repent and confess. In contrast to repent, to confess might not carry little or any meaning of sorrow or regret. When our children were young,

I would ask my son if he had pulled his sister's hair. He would quite honestly admit that he had done so. However, I did not sense any regret or sorrow and I sometimes thought that he might be thinking to himself that as soon as I turned my back he might do it again. In the New Testament, though, confession carries much of the same sense as repent. So when John tells us to confess our sin, he is also saying that we agree with God and that we are a sinner. That is not as easy as it sounds, is it? Have you ever found yourself justifying your sin to God? "Well, Lord, I didn't really mean to do it, but I was under a lot of stress." "I know what I did was wrong, but the other person really provoked me into it."

Repentance and confession of our sin before God offers no mea culpa or extenuating circumstances. We must acknowledge our sin plainly and clearly and accept responsibility. Remember Ephesians 2:8, "For by grace you are saved through *faith?*" We can repent of our sins, but there must be an act of faith. We must believe that Jesus is who he said he is and that he has the power to forgive us and make us a new creation. Our faith can spring from the certainty that Jesus *gospeloves* us and in fact has died for us. Paul states it well in his letter to the Romans in chapter 10, verses 9-10, "That if you confess with your mouth, 'Jesus is Lord', and believe in your heart that God raised him from the dead, you will be saved. For it is with your heart that you believe and are justified, and it is with your mouth that you confess and are saved." Again, we must allow for some cultural differences in the way we use certain words.

The Bible defines faith as "being sure of what we hope for and certain of what we do not see." Faith and belief are often used in much the same way in Scripture. They are both action words. Approximately 96 percent of all Americans believe that God exists. For a great percentage of those same people, this belief has no impact on how they live their daily lives. "Gospel light" brings us to the point of confessing our sins, but is not too concerned that we really believe in our heart that Jesus died for our sins and was raised from the dead, and by the power of the resurrection, we can become new creations in Christ Jesus. This is not something new. James, the brother of Jesus, addresses this issue in his New Testament letter. Chapter 2, verse 14 says, "What good is it, my brothers, if a man claims to have faith but has no deeds? Can such faith save him?" Verse 17 goes on to say, "In the same way, faith by itself, if it is not accompanied by action, is dead." I believe as a result of "gospel light", we have a lot of dead faith throughout America. Many people have said the right words, but the faith they have expressed is a mental acknowledgement rather than a saving faith. A faith that begins with the overwhelming, amazing, lavishing *gospelove* of Jesus has every possibility of becoming a "live" faith.

What are we saved for? "Gospel light" is primarily concerned that we are forgiven and have a place in heaven. Again, though, God has "so much more' in store for us. We have seen that the prevailing wind of God is a reconciling, *gospelove* wind. He is in the process of reconciling all things in the heavens and on the earth unto Himself through what Jesus Christ did on the cross; namely, reconciling a sinful creation, including us, to a holy God. The perspective of "gospel light", *naturalove,* is that the reconciling wind is blowing in the opposite direction. *Naturalove* sees the reconciling wind blowing to reconcile God to man. In other words, we make God in our own image and bring Him into our world where we can explain Him, understand Him, and have Him at our beck and call to help us when we need Him. *Gospelove* is all about God reconciling sinful man and the rest of the creation that has been stained by sin, unto Himself, the holy, righteous God. We come to God on His terms rather than trying to make Him in our own image. Many of the Bible passages that we try and use, we have approached through the lens of *naturalove* rather than *gospelove.* We are saved in the context of God's reconciling wind, not ours. We have looked at what we are saved from and how we are saved, but included in that must be what we are saved to. For most of us, we would just think of heaven as that is the emphasis of "gospel light".

Ephesians 2:10 captures the essence when it says, "For we are God's workmanship, created in Christ Jesus to do good works, which God prepared in advance for us to do." When we become new creations in Christ Jesus, we enter the kingdom of God and become citizens of this kingdom (Philippians 3:20). As citizens, we take our place in this kingdom and join with God as He purposes to establish His kingdom over all creation. God has prepared good works for us to do even before the foundation of the world. In other words, as a new creation in Christ, God will use you in His great plan of redemption for all things and He has created specific ways He is going to blow His reconciling wind through you and your life. When we begin to think of this, we most likely react by saying either to ourselves or God, "But I am not called to be a pastor, missionary, or evangelist." No matter, because God wants to use us in our everyday, ordinary lives. The good works He has for us is often in our marriage, in our family, in our jobs, in our neighborhoods. This is where we become his witnesses as we read in Acts 1:8. Paul has another word for it in 2 Corinthians 5:20, "We are therefore God's ambassadors, as though God makes his appeal through us." How do we get there? Well, let's take that journey together.

ALL YOU NEED IS LOVE

For Christ's love compels us, because we are convinced that one died for all, and therefore all died. And He died for all, that those who live should no longer live for themselves, but for him who died for them and was raised again. (2 Corinthians 5:14-15)

As I mentioned in the introduction, nearly everyone, believer and follower of Christ or non- believer, would agree with the statement that we should "love our neighbor". Jesus taught us a parable about the kind of *gospelove* He was talking about. The parable is called the story of the "Good Samaritan". (Luke 11:25-37) The term "good Samaritan" has woven its way into our common vernacular as there are organizations who use the word "Samaritan" in their title, but have little to do with the gospel and message of Jesus Christ. The story, or what we think of as the story, has something of a sentimental touch in our references. However, as Jesus told this story, his audience was mostly the religious leaders of the day. (Luke 11:25) It is difficult for us to understand the relationship between the Jewish leaders of the time and the Samaritans.

Samaria was one of the provinces of the nation of Israel and when the Babylonian empire came and basically destroyed Israel and took many captives, the people from Samaria remained steadfast and would not go with their captors. So, the Babylonians sent their own people to live among and control the Samaritans. As they did so, they (the Babylonians) and the Samaritans intermarried, brought their own pagan religion and syncretized that with the Samaritan's religion. When the Babylonian captivity ended and the Israelites returned to their own land, they despised the Samaritans and called them half-breeds and pagans. They considered them unclean, so the Israelites could not touch a Samaritan and would not even go through their land or be in their presence. The hatred and contempt were deep and binding. So, the very thought that Jesus put forth that a Samaritan would stop to help an Israelite on the road was not even something that the Israelites could contemplate, let alone do. The question that the religious leader asked in verse 29 is one that we all have to consider, "But he wanted to justify himself, so he asked Jesus, 'And who is my neighbor?'" This religious leader would have never given a thought that a Samaritan was included in that commandment. So, how about us? Who would we consider our neighbor?

Earlier, we looked at the verse in Luke 6:27-28 where Jesus says, "But to you who are listening I say: Love (*gospelove*) your enemies, do good to those who hate you, bless those who curse you, pray for those who mistreat you." How can we do that? Remember, our default definition of love comes from *naturalove,* which begins and ends with us. It always involves some kind of attraction, feeling, emotion, or kinship to generate some kind of "love". So, let's be honest with ourselves: If we have an enemy, designated either by the enemy or by us, we are not likely to ever have the "warm fuzzies" for them. What happens is even if we have some inclination to "love" them by doing "good to those who hate us", we will feel guilty, even hypocritical because we do not really "feel" love. How, then, do we reconcile the words of Jesus as a *command* to love. *Naturalove* cannot be commanded as it must be tied to some kind of self-interest, feeling, emotion, or kinship. The Great Commandment is just that, though, a commandment. Love (*gospelove*) the Lord your God with all of your heart, soul, mind, and strength and love (*gospelove*) your neighbor as yourself. Again, how can we do this?

Three days after we had moved to Goma, Zaire (now the Democratic Republic of Congo), the border between Rwanda and Congo closed. The house we lived in was within ten minutes walking to the border and crossing over to the Rwandan town of Gisenyi. Goma and Gisenyi could have been just one city, but a country border ran through it, a border that was arbitrarily drawn in a board room in Europe. The reason for the border closing was because some Rwandan refugees living in Uganda and some in Tanzania, had come into Rwanda with what they called "guerilla warfare. They would attack a village or town, do some looting and burning and then leave the country as soon as possible. The border remained closed for almost six months and it did make communication with our Rwandan church leaders difficult. Finally, though, the border reopened and there was more freedom of movement.

In light of this, the leaders planned a combined meeting of several churches on either side of the border to the north of Goma/Gisenyi. Several hundred people gathered for an open air church service. Since we had not been able to be together during the recent days, we dug a pit and filled it with water from a nearby creek and baptized a significant number of people. We also had baby dedications and the official recognition of members into the various churches there and the denomination. Though we had very little in the way of instruments (what we had were home made variations of some kind of drum) the singing was loud, exuberant, and joyful. I had the privilege of bringing the message from the Word and at the conclusion of the message, I invited those who wanted to become a new creation in Christ to come forward. Over twenty-five people made their way to the front and I prayed with them to open their hearts to Jesus the Christ and become followers of Him. When I finished, I sat down on the makeshift chair of a bale of hay with some kind of cover on it. Needless to say, I was tired and waited for the leaders to close the service. However, Pastor Andre from Rwanda told me that we were going to worship with more singing and I should stand up and join them. So, I did, and what happened next was a life changing moment for me that is still impacting me all these year later.

As I looked out at that sea of faces, the Holy Spirit began to speak to me even with the loud, exuberant singing that was taking place. In those faces, I saw genuine joy and hope and suddenly realized that there really was no earthly reason for that joy and hope. You see, as the Holy Spirit began to show me, these people lived in a situation that not only provided no hope, but there was little if any possibility that things could or would get better (they have not) any time in the future. Not one single person had driven or ridden in a car to get to the service. Some of them risked a border crossing because travel between the two countries was still difficult. When they left to go home, what would they be going to? Most of their houses would have been without a floor, only dirt. Only a very few would have electricity. Even fewer would have running water and probably none had indoor plumbing. Obviously, with no electricity, there were no TV's or even radios, though there might have been a few radios powered by batteries, though batteries were scarce and expensive. They would have little food in a pantry and would consider what to eat for tomorrow when tomorrow came. Their closets were mostly empty as they wore the same clothes most every day. They had little, if any access to medicine or medical help. There were a few clinics scattered about, but they were ill-equipped and scarcely staffed. Life expectancy at that time was 47 years of age. As the Spirit guided me through this litany, I looked again at their faces as they sang and danced with joy. I could feel the ground shaking from their movement. How could they? As I thought of their life and then thought of my life and all of the advantages of the world that I had or had access to, a question came to my mind, heart, and soul that has never left and is not simply answered. As the singing continued, I asked the Lord, "Lord, do you love me more than these?" I did not choose to be born in America, just as these folks did not choose to be born in this part of Africa. Until that moment, I had always thought the "things" of this world were blessings from God, you know, *God bless America.*

46

How could I say to any one of those worshipers, "God loves you"? What evidence of His love could I find in that setting?

How could I say "God bless you"? What evidence of His blessing was there in these people's lives? Over the course of the years since that revelation from God, I have had to continually go back there, relive that moment, then seek God, His Word, His Kingdom, and His presence. It has not been an easy journey and I have not crossed the finish line, but God is faithful and He has helped me to see and know His *gospelove* and realize where His true blessings are to be found.

Let's look again at the verse we read at the beginning of this chapter, 2 Corinthians 5:14-15. "For Christ's love (*gospelove)* compels us, because we are convinced that one died for all, and therefore all died. And he died for all, that those who live should no longer live for themselves but for him who died for them and was raised again. Webster's dictionary defines compel "to drive or urge forcefully or irresistibly." It carries the sense that "I can't help myself, I just have to do it." So, let me ask you, is there anything in your life that you are compelled to do? If so, what is the driving force behind that compulsion? When it comes to *gospelove,* what is the driving force that allows us to come to the same place as Paul and say, "Christ's love *compels* me"? The driving force for Paul is in the second part of verse 14, "because we are *convinced that one died for all."* Think about that word, "convinced" for a moment. That is also where we get the word "conviction". One of the dictionary definitions of the word "conviction" is "a strong persuasion or belief or the state of being convinced." In my experience interacting with people over the years, I think most people act on their convictions.

We have many preferences and we may think these preferences are convictions, but they never really result in consistent action.

Let me share an example. Most of us have at some time or another started some kind of diet or exercise program to get into shape. More often than not, these have not been very successful. When I hear people say something like, "I'm trying to watch what

I eat," I conclude they will not be very successful at losing any weight. They have responded to some emotion, perhaps a good look in the mirror, but just watching what they eat is not likely to produce the desired results. We all know it is difficult to change eating habits and to add exercise to our daily lifestyle. Some do it, however. They see it through and achieve the desired result. What is the difference? They have a conviction, a powerful persuasion that they must change. That kind of conviction can come from various sources, but that conviction keeps them going even when they are discouraged or do not feel like it.

As we began our ministry in Rwanda and Congo, I recall a particular moment when God revealed His plan to me. I was in a meeting with Pastor Tombo and Pastor Andre and was sharing with them how we would work together in the development of the ministry in these two countries. The model I had seen in missionaries in Africa was that the missionary was in charge and the nationals would work for them. God seemed to be pointing me in a different direction. I seemed to hear Him say, "Do you really trust me to build my church in Rwanda and Congo?" I realized that I needed to empower these two leaders and be a catalyst for them and mentor them as they lead the work. I shared with them in that meeting that they were the leaders and I would come alongside them and resource them and help them, but they were the leaders.

While they sometimes made their own mistakes, we continued to work through them and other leaders that God provided. It seemed, as I look back, that that decision allowed the wind of the Spirit to blow, as we could barely keep up with the growth. While I hoped these men learned something from me, I know I learned much from them. After living in Congo for a year, the political situation in Rwanda and Eastern Congo continued to worsen and it was no longer safe to live there, so we moved to Nairobi, Kenya, where our field office was located. I traveled to Rwanda and Congo as often as I could and continued to be amazed at how the Lord was moving in developing the church. One night, I received a telephone call from Pastor Andre, who was now our district superintendent in Rwanda. Phone calls were often difficult, but we had a good connection and Andre told me of the situation in the southern part of the country where the rains were late and famine was beginning to be experienced. He asked me if there was any way I could get help, especially for the pastors in that area. The next day, I contacted our Compassionate Ministries global office, and we set in motion to get some relief to that area. However, that was going to take a little while for all the wheels to turn. I was able to visit Rwanda a short time later and I did not hear Andre say anything about the pastors in the southern area. As I talked to some of the other leaders, they shared with me that Andre had sold several of his cows to get money to buy food for his pastors. I had to ask myself if I was compelled enough by the *gospelove* of Christ to do the same thing.

When we try to enter the kingdom through "gospel light," then how convinced are we that the way we live makes much difference? We create a few preferences, perhaps even attending church or minor lifestyle changes, but we are not really living by conviction. When we really look at the above verse, though, we can begin to realize that all convictions flow out of one: *Christ died for me.* Think about that. Do you believe that? Do you really believe Jesus died in your place, for your sin? Do you really believe that was necessary? Do you think God had to go that far to reconcile us to Him? Does it sometimes just become a throwaway phrase that you use in church or perhaps sing the words in a song? What does it really mean to be convinced that Jesus died for us?

Acts 2:42 says, "They committed themselves to the teaching of the apostles, the life together, the common meal, and the prayers." (The Message) We strived to be an Acts 2:42 church: Using ACTS as an acronym, we can focus on four key components of life in the church. Authentic worship (the common meal), Committed community (the life together), Transforming mission (teaching of apostles), Serving (through a life of prayer). Let us focus on authentic worship for a moment. What do you think of when you think of worship? If you attend church, you probably think of music. You can envision people singing songs of praise and devotion to God. Depending on the style of worship in your church, you probably think of people responding in some expression along with the music. Do you consider the other components of the "worship" service as worship? How about prayer? Do you consider the offering, where you might give money to the church (hopefully that is to God), as an act of worship? What about the sermon? Is that worship?

You might ask how we translate the common meal as mentioned in Acts 2:42 as authentic worship? If you read the paragraph containing verses 42-47, you will discover a description of life in the newly formed church of Jesus Christ. The common meal or breaking of bread referred to the Lord's Supper or communion as most people know it. They also ate meals together, but they also shared the communion meal together on a regular basis. What is the purpose of the Lord's Supper? When Jesus shared the bread and cup with his disciples shortly before his death, He told them to share this with other believers by saying, "Do this in remembrance of me" (1 Corinthians

11:24). What did He want us to remember? Through the elements of the bread, His body, and the cup, His blood, He wanted us to call attention to the sacrificial death He suffered in our place. He wanted to take us to the cross. Authentic worship will always lead us to the cross. It might be in a song, or a prayer, or in the sermon, or even in bringing our tithes and offerings to the Lord. It might be in all of these, or in the experience of the communion meal, but when we come to the cross, we cannot escape the reality that Jesus died for us. If we truly consider the cross, we cannot help but be humbled by the reality that Jesus died for us, for all men. The redemptive love of God (*gospelove*) speaks loudly at that moment and we can begin to be compelled by that love because we are convinced that He died for us.

Now, you might say, worship is also for celebration and inspiration. Without a doubt! From a humble reverence to exuberant praise becomes an expression of what we know, the *conviction* deep within us that Jesus died for us and we know that this changes everything. We can now be on the journey because, as Paul says in 2 Corinthians 5:15, "And he died for all, that those who live should no longer live for themselves, but for him who died for them and was raised again." In the light of the cross, our focus becomes Jesus and what He has done for us and what He is doing and we can make a choice of the will to obey His commandment. If *naturalove* is based on human reactions, emotions, feelings, and attractions, is *gospelove* just an act of the will of God and does He not have any feelings, emotions, or attractions to us? As we have seen in the Scriptures, *gospelove* comes from God. The powerful declaration in Romans 5:8 states, "But God demonstrates his own love *(gospelove)* for us in this: While we were still sinners, Christ died for us." In John chapter 4, Jesus has an encounter with a Samaritan woman, which was highly unusual as we have seen in the parable of the good Samaritan. Among other things, Jesus talks to her about worship

51

and He says, "Yet a time is coming and has now come when the true worshipers will worship the Father in the Spirit and in truth, for they are the kind of worshipers the Father seeks. God is spirit and his worshipers must worship in the Spirit and in truth." (John 4:23-24) Worshipping the Lord in Spirit or in the Spirit means that we are engaged in the deepest levels of our heart and our life. That includes our emotions, feelings, attractions, and joys. Not only do we worship God in this way, but He meets us in those places as He even knows our groaning. Our *gospelove* relationship with God through Christ is not just a robotic response to *gospelove* someone who is unlovable, but it is a rich, deep, experience that is beyond anything we can know from this world.

As we have seen, 2 Corinthians 5:17 says, "Therefore, if anyone is in Christ, he is a new creation; the old has gone, the new has come!" Think about that for a moment. A new creation in Christ Jesus. The old has gone, the new has come. So what is the old that has gone and the new that has come? Jesus gives us a picture in John 13:34-

35. He has just shared the last supper with his disciples. He has, to their astonishment, washed their feet. Judas walked out to betray him. Then he says, "A new command I give you: Love *gospelove* one another. As I have *gospeloved* you, so you must also *gospelove* one another. By this all men will know that you are my disciples, if you *gospelove* one another. The words "love one another" were not new to the disciples. They were found in Leviticus and were well-known to the Israelites. In fact, many Jewish men wore those words in what they called phylacteries, either on their forehead or on their arm. It would be like a small pouch and inside would be the words of Scripture; often this Scripture would be to love God and love your neighbor. So why did Jesus say this was a new command?

The meaning was now made known through Jesus and his actions. He had washed their feet; he was going to die in their place. "As I have *gospeloved* you, you must *gospelove* one another," Jesus says. This was what made it new. So when we have come to the cross and been confronted with the incredible reality that Jesus died for us, we can let go of the old, which is the self-centered life (*naturalove*) we have all lived. What becomes new is the compelling *gospelove* of Christ that says we should no longer live for ourselves, but for him who died for us and was raised again. This is why worship is so central to who we are in Christ. The centerpiece of our worship is Jesus, the cross and the common meal or the Lord's Supper. It is there that we see the overwhelming and humbling reality that Jesus died for us. When we truly face the cross, there is nothing of ourselves there; rather, it is Jesus that we see. The more we are convinced (conviction) of this, the more we are capable of being compelled by the *gospelove* of Christ.

Worship, then, is more than just the corporate worship that takes place when we come together with other believers and engage in worship together. That is important, even vital, for our experience in Christ. However, I believe Jesus calls us to worship as a lifestyle. If you read Acts 2:42-47, you will discover that worship was central to their very life together. How, though, do we even begin to make worship a lifestyle in the twenty-first century? Is it really possible in our busy, hectic, even frantic pace of life? I truly believe it is possible and really holds the key on our journey to living out being a new creation in Christ Jesus, an ambassador through whom God makes His appeal. As I grew up in the church and even into the first ten to fifteen years of ministry, I gave little thought or attention to worship. Oh, we had a "worship" service at 11:00 AM on Sundays, but mostly we had what we called the "preliminaries", which would be to sing a couple of hymns, give some announcements, include a prayer, take the offering, and maybe a "special" solo by someone in the congregation. These were all preparing for the big moment, the moment when I could deliver the sermon that would change the world (still trying to come up with that one). In reading the Old Testament, though, I began to see that every place an "offering" would be given, it was considered "worship". The difficulties the Israelites had in keeping the covenant with God almost always was a matter of worship. In the last book of the Old Testament, Malachi, God presents the people of Israel with strong rebukes that have to do with their worship and their offerings. "But you profane (the name of the Lord) it. When you bring injured, lame or diseased animals and offer them as sacrifices, should I accept them from your hands?" says the Lord. (Malachi 1:12-13) Many of you know the story of Cain and Abel, when Cain murdered his brother. The issue was worship and offering to the Lord. We read in Genesis 4:3, "In the course of time Cain brought some of the fruits of the soil as an offering to the Lord. And Abel also brought an offering—fat portions from some of the firstborn of his flock. The Lord looked with favor on Abel and his offering, but on Cain and his offering he did not look with favor." What was the difference? Abel brought his best and Cain just tried to get by with what he could bring.

Let us return to Malachi. God says to the Israelites that they have turned away from his decrees and have not kept the terms of covenant that God has established. So, He says to them, "Return to me, and I will return to you. But you ask, 'How are we to return?' But you ask, 'How are we to return?' Will a mere mortal rob God? Yet you rob me. But you ask, 'How are we robbing you?' In tithes and offerings. You are under a curse—your whole nation—because you are robbing me. Bring the whole tithe into the storehouse." (Malachi 3:7-10) In chapter one, God tells the people that they are basically cheating God as they bring lame and diseased animals for sacrifice. However we may define worship or think of worship, the clear message through the Bible is that we bring God the very best. When I began to see this principle as it pertained to corporate worship and a lifestyle of worship, my whole perspective began to change and that process of change continues each day.

How do we begin to think of a lifestyle of worship? Do we just walk around singing praise choruses all of the time? A passage of Scripture that has greatly helped me to begin this journey is found in Romans 12:1-2, which describes a lifestyle of worship. Let's look together at what it says: "Therefore, I urge you brothers and sisters, in view of God's mercy, to offer your bodies as living sacrifices, holy and pleasing to God—this is your spiritual act of worship. Do not conform any longer to the pattern of this world, but be transformed by the renewing of your mind. Then you will be able to test and approve what God's will is—his good, pleasing and perfect will." As we mentioned, when you read the Old Testament, you will see that when the people of Israel, God's covenant people, were involved in worship in that they always brought an offering to God. Many times, this offering would be a sacrificial animal, anywhere from a dove to a lamb. When Jesus died on the cross, the sacrificial Lamb of God, no more sacrifices of animals or burnt offerings were required. Hebrews 10:10 says, "We have been made holy through the sacrifice of the body of Jesus Christ once for all." Verse 12 follows, "But when this priest (Christ Jesus) had offered for all time one sacrifice for sins, he sat down at the right hand of God." And then verse14, "Because by one sacrifice he has made perfect forever those who are being made holy."

So if the supreme sacrifice has been made and there are no more burnt offerings we can bring to God, how do we approach Him in worship? First, we have to come through Jesus Christ, who sits at the right hand of God. We must believe, be convinced, that He died for us and rose again, conquering sin and death. Then, we bring ourselves, our bodies, our lives as *living sacrifices*. What does this mean? We can gain insight into this in the Message version of Romans 12:1, "So, here's what I want you to do, God helping you. Take your everyday, ordinary life—and place it before God as an offering." Our lifestyle of worship is all about our daily routines. We must, though, intentionally and willfully offer those to God as our spiritual worship, service, and ministry. God has a redemptive purpose in our marriage, in our family, in our jobs, in how we spend our money, in our relationships with colleagues and neighbors. Romans 12:2 in the Message reads, "Don't become so well-adjusted to your culture that you fit into it without even thinking. Instead, *fix your attention on God*. You will be changed from the inside out. Your life will become an expression of *gospelove*. Readily recognize what He wants from you, and quickly respond to it. Unlike the culture around you, always dragging you down to its level of immaturity, God brings the best out of you, develops well-formed maturity in you."

Fixing our attention on God is not that easy in a busy, distracting world, is it? I read of a man who was struggling in this area. He would pray first thing in the morning to be used by God during the day. Then, he would get to work, get busy, and realize at the end of the day that he had not been consciously fixing his attention on God at all. He asked God to help him and God gave him inspiration. He worked in a large office for an oil company. He was at a management level, but he could see across the building from his office. He began to consciously build keys into his routine. When he went to the drinking fountain (remember those?) for a drink of water, he would look at a fellow worker and begin to pray for him, whether he knew him or not. When he took a coffee break, he would do the same thing. Amazingly, after a couple of weeks of doing this every day, people started coming to him and asking him spiritual questions or if he could pray for them. He then began a Bible study in his office during lunch. People would bring a brown bag lunch and they would share the Scripture. God began to open up many opportunities of ministry that were all around him and that he had not seen until he began to *fix his attention on God.*

So, are you convinced (*conviction*) Jesus died for you? Does this conviction compel you with the *gospelove* of Christ? Are you ready to begin a lifestyle of worship? In order to continue our journey, we need to not only fix our attention on God, but also we need to bring our life into focus, God's focus.

THE WORLD ACCORDING TO JESUS

So, from now on we regard no one from a worldly point of view. Though we once regarded Christ in this way, we do so no longer. (2 Corinthians 5:16)

Perspective. A dictionary definition of "perspective" states, "The interrelation in which a subject or its parts are mentally viewed." Another way to view it is to think of perspective as the lens through which we see things. Surprisingly, or maybe not, we do not all have the same lens. In fact, the lens through which you see the world is unique; there is no one else that has exactly the same perspective on everything that you do. Hold it! Wait a minute! I know what you are thinking. If everyone had the same perspective on the world as you, it would be a perfect world, right? So how does this happen? Everything you experience; everything that happens to you, everything that you learn all contribute to your experience. No one has walked in exactly the same shoes as you, so your perspective is unique. Our perspective is a constantly changing, moving lens. Some things in there are rigid, sure, but we have new experiences, reactions, and knowledge every day. All of those things change the focus of our lens, even though we may not always be aware of those changes.

When Paul (who wrote the 2 Corinthian letter) mentions our "worldly point of view," he is talking about perspective. What is a worldly point of view? Simply put, it is the lens of the sinful nature that we inherited from Adam. Remember when we looked at Adam and Eve and how everything changed changed when they disobeyed

God? Their perspective, their lens through which they saw God, was radically changed. They had enjoyed wonderful fellowship, almost a partnership with God in His plan to redeem and reconcile the earth to Him. They were living in the covenant and they were open and transparent with God. Then, after their disobedience, they were afraid and fearful. Why? I believe they knew and had experienced the holiness and righteousness of God as well as His *gospelove.* When they became aware of their sin, they were afraid because they no longer could stand to be in the presence of His holiness. Their perspective of God and the world changed considerably. They were now looking through the lens of sin nature.

Their first thought was to clothe themselves. Their lives began to be lived as man-centered rather than God-centered. Our first mission assignment was in the country of the Netherlands. We went there from seminary to be part of a team led by a Dutch pastor to plant a church in the city of Rotterdam. I did not realize how Americanized my world view was until I lived in another country. I also did not realize how my own understanding of the gospel was looking through the lens of American culture rather than Scripture. Return with me to the church meeting on the border of Rwanda and Congo when I was faced with the question "Does God love me more than these?" I was born a white male in the United States of America. I had no say in that, but as I experienced other places and cultures, I realized that my status opened practically every advantage this world has to offer. So, did God love me more than these Africans? By every conceivable measure that this world knows, the answer would have to be yes. They had no hope. The time we lived in Congo, we and they experienced 4,000 per cent inflation. I know that sounds impossible, but that is how it was. The only way we could survive that is that we were paid in dollars and were therefore not as subject to the local economy. How, then, could these people love a God who seemingly condemned them to such a hopeless existence? As I got to know them and lived and worshiped among them, I realized that as they became new creations in Christ Jesus, God changed their perspective from hopelessness to hope and their world view became much more of an eternal context than mine or most Americans. They do have a hope and they know that it lies in the kingdom of God as God reconciles all things in the heavens and on the earth unto Himself. I began to see that most of the things I thought of as "blessings" were really responsibilities. In the parable of the talents, did Jesus love one more than the other because he gave them different amounts? No, the question is what did we do with what we have? To whom much is given, much is required, says Jesus.

Look again at David in Psalm 51. In verse 5, he says, "Surely I was sinful at birth, sinful from the time my mother conceived me. Surely you desire truth in the inner parts." David is talking about perspective as he knows that he cannot see clearly until he can be free from the sin he inherited at birth. He cannot see from the lens of truth in his inner being until he undergoes a radical change. So, he cries out in verse 10, "Create in me a pure heart, O God, and renew a steadfast spirit within me." This steadfast, or right, spirit will be a new perspective on God, truth, and himself. This pure heart will also allow him to receive, live in, and give the *gospelove* of Jesus. He knew what this perspective was going to be when he could see the world from God's point of view. He says in verse 13, "Then I will teach transgressors your ways, and sinners will turn back to you." Then he says in verse 15, "O, Lord, open my lips and my mouth will declare your praise." David realized that this new creation would give him a kingdom viewpoint; that he would have a lifestyle of worship and he would live for others in a redemptive lifestyle.

Gospelove!

Remember 2 Corinthians 5:17, "Therefore, if anyone is in Christ, he is a new creation; the old has gone, the new has come!" The old man-centered focus is replaced by a God-centered lens. Do not forget, though, where all of this starts. ***Conviction!*** The conviction that Christ died for us moves us in the direction of God's perspective. Look again at Romans 12:2 in the Message, "Fix your attention on God. You'll be changed from the inside out." Your perspective on God, the world, you, and your purpose will change. The NIV says it this way, "Be transformed by the renewing of your mind. Then you will be able to test and approve what God's will is—his good, pleasing and perfect will." In other words, as we see life through the lens of the compelling, redeeming *gospelove* of God, the ways and purposes of God become much clearer. The reason the will of God is so often hard to see, understand, accept, and obey is because we are still looking through the wrong lens.

"Gospel light" is primarily concerned with forgiveness of sins and a ticket to heaven, but not much with the lens of God. So as we continue to look at life through a man-centered perspective, we become the proverbial tail that wags the dog. Give me this, bless me with that, heal me, prosper me, make me happy we demand of God. It is not that God does not want to do those things for us; it is that we do not see His purpose in and through our lives. Without this perspective, we are always going to get it wrong when we come to the word *gospelove*. So we get angry and disappointed with God, though we would rarely admit to this. We are still looking at life through a worldly point of view as Paul puts it. Paul mentions that he once regarded Christ that way. When he was Saul, he was a very religious man, a devout Jew. He saw Jesus as a threat to his religion and way of life, so he wanted to get rid of anything or anyone that had anything to do with Jesus. Then, on the road to Damascus to carry out his war against Jesus, he is confronted by the crucified, resurrected Christ. Saul is confronted by the cross, the reality that Jesus died for him, and he is completely changed, made a new creation. His focus changes from a worldly point of view to a mind of Christ perspective.

Philippians 2:5-8 sheds more light on a Christ perspective of God, life, *gospelove,* and the world. "Your attitude should be the same as that of Christ Jesus: Who, being in very nature God, did not consider equality with God something to be grasped, but made himself nothing, taking the very nature of a servant, being made in human likeness. And being found in appearance as a man, he humbled himself and became obedient to death—even death on a cross." The word "attitude" in verse 5 literally means to think. The King James Version said, "Let this mind be in you." We should think of ourselves in the same way Christ thinks of himself as described in this passage. In a word, we are to think redemptive, Jesus being one with the Father, basking in glory we cannot yet imagine, voluntarily offers to come to earth and take the form of a man. Before we just pass that by and go on, please take note of verse 6, "Who, being in very nature God, did not consider equality with God as something to be grasped, but made himself nothing." Think for a moment of who you are in life. Anything you have achieved or earned in life that gives you definition or station, you want to hang on to and even let people know who you are. In fact, we are fairly tenacious when we feel we have earned or deserve something and others either do not want to recognize it or not give full credit for it.

What does it mean when Paul says that Jesus "made himself nothing"? A more literal translation is that Christ "emptied himself". What did He empty himself of? He did not empty himself of his deity. Colossians 1:19 says, "For God was pleased to have all his fullness dwell in him (Christ)." When He became incarnate, He was God in the flesh. The apostle John stated much the same thing in John 1:14, "The Word (Christ) became flesh and made his dwelling among us. We have seen his glory, the glory of the One and Only, who came from the Father, full of grace and truth." Jesus, when He was on the earth, was fully God and fully man. That being said, what did He lay aside in order to become not just a man, but a servant obedient to death? When we look at the big picture of what God is doing, "Through him (Christ) to reconcile to himself (God the Father) all things, whether things on earth or things in heaven, by making peace through his blood, shed on the cross," we can begin to get a glimpse of understanding of what Jesus emptied or laid aside. He gave up his rights that enjoyed in the glory of the Father's kingdom and at the Father's right hand.

If you read the gospel accounts of the life and ministry of Jesus as found in Matthew, Mark, Luke, and John, you will become aware of the difference in perspective of Jesus and His disciples. The disciples, like most Jews at the time, had their own vision of the Messiah, what he would do when he came and how he would do it. Yes, they talked in terms of the kingdom, but their viewpoint was not so much the kingdom of God as it was the kingdom of Israel. They believed the Messiah would reestablish Israel as the dominant kingdom in the world, just like in the good old days of David and Solomon, and they would no longer be under any oppression from Rome or anyone else. So when Jesus taught about the kingdom of God, they were thinking in terms of their own man-centered focus. This is also what we often do with "gospel light". We mix the teachings of (at least some of them) with the American dream and believe that God is there to help us reach that dream. It is not about God at all, but about us.

There are numerous occasions in the gospels that the disciples try to convince Jesus to use the force of the sword or some force to bring about this kingdom. They are often frustrated when He does not. Frankly, there are times when I am reading these accounts that I find myself in the same attitude as the disciples and I just want Jesus to "take care of his enemies".

When he was being crucified, people were mocking him. Would that be a time when we would want to strike back, to call on the angels of God's armies to come and wipe out the enemies? Listen to what the mockers had to say, "He saved others, but can't save himself! He's the king of Israel!

Let him come down now from the cross, and we will believe in him". (Matthew 27:42) Would that not have been tempting? It appears that right up until the time Jesus ascended to heaven, the disciples still had the wrong perspective. In Acts chapter 1, Jesus is giving last minute instructions for his disciples to stay in Jerusalem and they would be clothed in the Holy Spirit. The disciples were obviously not on the same page because they asked him, "Lord, are you at this time going to restore the kingdom to Israel?" (Acts 1:6) In other words, are you finally going to be the Messiah we think you should be and establish the nation and the kingdom of Israel? I think Jesus must have thought about giving up, but he patiently described to them what they would become—his ambassadors (Acts 1:8).

So we are to have the same attitude, mindset, or perspective as Jesus. He was totally committed to the way of the cross as he became a servant obedient to death. His sacrificial death was going to reconcile everything in the heavens and on the earth unto Himself. In order for us to have the same perspective, we have to believe that we also have to journey by the way of the cross. What does that mean to us? We do not have to die a sacrificial death as Jesus has done this once and for all (Hebrews 9:28). We do need to experience crucifixion, however. Romans 6:6 states, "For we know that our old self was crucified with him so that the body of sin might be done away with, that we should no longer be slaves to sin." Our testimony should parallel that of Paul in Galatians 2:20, "I have been crucified with Christ and I no longer live, but Christ lives in me." Later in Galatians 5:24 we read, "Those who belong to Christ Jesus have crucified the sinful nature with its passions and desires." How does this crucifixion come about? We must surrender our rights in the same way Jesus did when He went to the cross. When Pilate was questioning Jesus, Jesus answered, "My kingdom is from another place." Jesus could have used the right He had as the one and only Son of the Father, but He emptied himself of those rights in order to be redemptive.

As Americans, this is a difficult step to take. Actually, it is difficult for anyone who is led by the sin nature. "Gospel light" does not ask or demand that we give up anything. In fact, we only get or receive. We receive forgiveness of sins and eternal life. Jesus did all the work; what we receive is by grace. We have even become so clever that we convince ourselves that to give up anything smacks of works and we are treading on the gospel of grace. Remember, though, what we are saved from, how we are saved, and what we are saved to. In America, we have a bill of rights as part of our Constitution. I have lived in other countries where rights are not guaranteed and are often trampled on by those in authority. So believe me when I say I am grateful for what we have in the United States of America. Think about it, though. If our rights are constitutionally guaranteed, how do we respond to God's call to empty ourselves of our rights and not live for ourselves, but for the One who died for us? This is the heart of *gospelove*. It is always about others; it is always redemptive. Perhaps it would help us to see some examples of what Jesus means when He says his kingdom is not of this world.

If you really want to begin to see, hear, and feel the essence of the kingdom God, read the gospel of Matthew chapters 5-7. This is referred to as the Sermon on the Mount, but it is much more than a sermon. This is the foundation of *gospelove* and the message of the gospel of Jesus the Christ. Again, we can become very clever when self interest is our major concern. Through the eyes of our sin nature dominated perspective, many have explained away the import of these chapters by rationalizing that the Sermon on the Mount is indeed about the kingdom of God, but a future kingdom when we go to heaven. However, at the very beginning of his ministry, Jesus says, "Repent, for the kingdom of heaven is near" (Matthew 4:17). He often refers to the kingdom of God, or heaven, as being near, at hand, and among us. In other words, He was bringing the kingdom to us as a present reality. So in Matthew 6:33, Jesus tells us to "seek first his kingdom and his righteousness, and all these things will be given to you as well." "These things" are the things of the kingdom of this world He has just been talking about in verses 25-32. It is obvious that He wants us to focus our lens of perspective on the reality of the kingdom of God, even while we are in this world.

How important is this redemptive perspective? In Matthew 6:43, we read the words of Jesus, "You have heard that it was said, 'Love your neighbor and hate your enemy.' But I tell you: Love your enemies and pray for those who persecute you." In Matthew 5:11, He says, "Blessed are you when people insult you, persecute you and falsely say all kinds of evil against you because of me. Rejoice and be glad, because great is your reward in heaven, for in the same way they persecuted the prophets who were before you." We referred earlier to similar words of Jesus in Luke 6:27-28, "But I tell you who hear me: Love your enemies, do good to those who hate you, bless those who curse you, pray for those who mistreat you." These statements are all about *gospelove*. *Gospelove* will not be possible for us without the redemptive perspective. Without the *gospelove* of Jesus being lavished on us, we could not respond to those situations just mentioned in such a manner that is described. If we exercise our rights in those instances, we would probably loudly proclaim that we have been wronged and demand that our rights to justice, retribution, perhaps even revenge be fulfilled. Now, think about Jesus. All those things and worse happened to him while He was here on earth and He had every right to exercise the authority He had as the Son of God. He could have called out for justice and retribution to those who insulted him, mocked him, beat him, and crucified him. I do not think He would have wrong or sinful to do so. It was his right, was it not? But what did he do? While hanging on the cross, He said, "Father, forgive them, for they do not know what they are doing" (Luke 23:34). Our immediate thought is, "Well, I'm not Jesus!" True enough, but Scripture says, "Your attitude should be the same as that of Christ Jesus" (Philippians 2:5).

Again, everything flows from worship. It is in and through authentic worship that I am confronted by the cross and the conviction that Jesus died for me. I can also be confronted by the reality that He died for my enemy, the one who insulted me, the one who lied about me, the one who perhaps is making my life miserable. When I can begin to see this person through the lens of Jesus, I see a bigger picture. Jesus died for this person as well. Before we respond according to our rights, we are to pray for this person (Luke 6:28). That prayer is perhaps more for us than it is for them, because the purpose of that prayer is to put that person in the light of the lens of Jesus, which happens to be a redemptive lens. Is this easy? Certainly not! Is it possible? Yes, because of the life of Christ in us, because we are new creations in Christ Jesus.

When we were finally ready to move to Goma, Congo, we needed to find a house. There were no rental agencies or real estate agents, so we had to use word of mouth to find a house. I made a trip to Goma to find a house without my wife being with me (big mistake!). I was staying in a hotel and became acquainted with the owner. I told him I was looking for a house and he said that he happened to own a house that was coming open. I went to look at the house, and while it was not something we would have considered in California, I did not see that we had a lot of options, so I told him I would take it. I went back to Kenya and a week or so later, LaVonna and I made our way to Goma. Our container with all of our furniture and goods was still making its way to Goma, so when we arrived, we had a house but no furniture and no car. When LaVonna first saw the house she burst into tears (they were not tears of joy), but after we had our furniture, she did what she always did and made it into a wonderful home. However, we were having trouble getting all the necessary permissions to get our container into the country, so I took LaVonna back to Nairobi and I went back to see if I could get our container into Congo.

I was staying in our house as the landlord had a chair and a bed put in it from the hotel, but that is all the furniture I had. After a few days, I was still trying to get our container in and was invited to the landlord's house for lunch. After lunch, he brought me back to the house and after a couple of hours I was not feeling too well. As the evening turned to night, I continued to feel worse and realized I needed some help. We had hired a guard and this was his first night on the job. I told him I was sick and asked him to go to the hotel and see if he could get some help as I knew no one else in town. The manager of the hotel came back with him and I told him I was very sick and I needed some help. He had a car and he told me he would try and find some medicine. After a short while he returned and told me he was taking me to a clinic. I was surprised there was such a thing and particularly at that hour, which was well past midnight. We arrived at a dark building which looked like a house and went inside. There were several ladies inside that he said were nurses.

They asked me what was wrong and I gave them my symptoms. They said I had malaria and they wanted to give me an injection. We had been warned about needles in our field orientation, but at that point I really did not care because I was so sick. They gave me three injections and after each shot, my whole body seemed to be seized up in a cramp, probably from dehydration. After the injections, the hotel manager took me home. After sleeping for a few hours, he came back and took me to the clinic where they gave me two more injections.

For most of the next week I lay in bed in that empty house. The hotel sent some soup down to the house each day so I could have something to eat. As I lay there, I began to complain to God. We had left everything to come to Africa and nothing had gone right, it seemed. Here I was lying in bed in an empty house with my wife in Nairobi, my two younger children in another part of Kenya at boarding school, and our oldest son back in California. No furniture, no car, and no family. This was not the way it was supposed to be. Were we really needed here anyway? Weren't there plenty of churches in Rwanda and Congo? Maybe this is all a big mistake. As I lay there, God began talking to me. Gently, of course. First, I became very aware that God does not appreciate whiners. Again, Jesus went to the cross in my place, so in light of that how could I ever complain about anything? Then He began to help me see that part of the world through His eyes, His redemptive lens. *Gospelove!* He asked me what our mission was as a church and I responded that we were committed to making Christlike disciples in the nations.

He then assured me that that is the reason we were there and he was going to do that through us and the church there in Rwanda and Congo. I felt peace and while all of our circumstances did not sort themselves out immediately, I was able to begin to see God's perspective and the reconciling wind of the Holy Spirit, *gospelove,* began to blow.

WRITTEN IN THE WIND

One of the first churches that began in Congo was in a village called Bulengo. We would refer to this church as the "banana leaf church". In that part of Eastern Congo, there were no paved roads once you left the town of Goma. So we would take a dirt road for several miles and then there was another road, difficult to find and to see, that turned off toward Lake Kivu. A short distance after turning on this road, we would drive into a thick forest or banana trees. We were leaving the rest of the world and entering into a secluded, isolated area. At least, that is what it felt like. After a few miles in the banana forest, we came upon a village, near the shore of the lake. I am sure that village is what many people picture in their minds what Africa is like. The huts were mostly mud and sticks, with grass and banana leaf roofs. In the center of the village was a little larger mud, stick, and banana leaf structure that was the church. The first time I went to that church, we came in an old taxi. Not many cars ever came to the village, so our arrival caused quite a commotion. They let us off and went back to Goma to pick up some others that were going to join us. In the meantime, the church service started and when it came time for the sermon, I was invited to preach. I was preaching with an interpreter, and just about the time we were in rhythm and into the message, the old taxi returned with the rest of the group. Suddenly, the entire congregation got up and went outside to see the car and who was in it. The other missionary with us asked me what I said that made everyone leave! After a few moments, their curiosity satisfied, they came back into the church and we continued the sermon.

The pastor of this banana leaf church was Pastor Bahavu. He was a very humble man, but he had a quiet strength about him. The chief of the village started coming to their church and as a result, they were given a prominent location in the center of the village.

After the service, the pastor and his wife invited us to their home to have something to eat before we went on to the next church. They lived in a typical hut with a dirt floor. It was rather dark inside and the other missionary was getting a bit anxious about what we might be offered to eat and if it would be safe. I told him not to worry, to accept it with thanksgiving, and ask the Lord to bless it. After eating, it was time for us to leave and as we stood up to go, I felt something moving around my feet. I looked and saw Pastor Bahavu down on his knees cleaning my shoes. I was so moved by his humility that I could hardly move.

Like most of the pastors there, every time I saw Pastor Bahavu, he was wearing the same shirt. The Lord revealed to me that I did not need all of the shirts I had, so I gave some of them to the pastors. I remember that every time I saw Pastor Bahavu after that, he was wearing the shirt that I gave him. After the genocide in Rwanda that spilled over into Eastern Congo, I heard from others that Pastor Bahavu lost his life trying to protect some people from the soldiers. He was one of many pastors we lost during that time, many of them in heroic service trying to protect and save not only their people, but anyone who was in danger. As I think about him, I realize that Pastor Bahavu was fulfilling the purpose for which God created him, called him, and equipped him. While the rest of the world outside of the "banana leaf" village may never have heard of him, he fulfilled the good works which God prepared in advance for him to do.

How often do you think to yourself, "Why am I here on this earth? Is there a purpose and meaning for me?" I believe most people contemplate those questions from time to time. It is probably also true that those are uncomfortable thoughts and questions, so rather than spending too much time thinking about our purpose, we do all we can to keep busy and active so we do not really have to think about it. When we think about our purpose in life we are most likely trying to define ourselves or our reason for being in almost everything we do. Even our addictions become a desperate cry either for meaning or to cover up our cries for purpose. Why are we like this? God created us for a purpose. As we saw earlier

Adam and Eve were God's creations to become His covenant people/partners to redeem the world and establish the kingdom of God. That purpose has not changed, and even though sin has seemed to mess things up, Christ has redeemed that purpose on the cross. He has made us new creations in Him. Now, He can fulfill what we are saved to or for. Ephesians 2:10 says, "For we are God's workmanship, created in Christ Jesus to do good works, which God prepared in advance for us to do."

That is an amazing statement. The word "workmanship" can also be thought of as a masterpiece. As new creations in Christ Jesus, we are God's masterpiece. The good works that God prepared in advance is difficult to grasp as we get caught up in God's infinity, but as God was and is reconciling all things unto Himself through what Christ did on the cross, He has put us in the equation. We all have a significant role to play in this eternal drama, even as we are a part of the redemption. We are still God's covenant people. That is important to remember. As it has been since the beginning, the covenant is dual-sided and we keep our side of the covenant by our obedience. He will be our God and we will be His people. Our purpose is wrapped in, around, and through that covenant.

Paul lays this out clearly in 2 Corinthians 5:18-19. As he once again states, God's overall purpose of reconciling all things in the heavens and on the earth unto Himself through what Christ did on the cross, he specifies what our, the creations in Christ, role is in this great redemptive plan. In verse 18, Paul declares that we have been given the ministry of reconciliation. In order to fulfill that role and that ministry, he says, "And he has *committed* to us the message of reconciliation." That is a strong statement, isn't it? I do not think he is just saying for us to consider this ministry and this message if we really want to, if we have time, if we think we can do it. Can you see the covenantal relationship in these statements? I will be your God. I am in the process of reconciling all things in the heavens and on the earth through what my Son, Jesus Christ, did on the cross, making peace through the shedding of His blood. You will be my people, my instruments, my *ambassadors* that I will bless, empower, and use to accomplish this redemptive plan.

As Paul summarizes this ministry and message that God has given to His new creations, he says, "We are Christ's ambassadors, as though God were making his appeal through us." I am not sure we have realized the importance and magnitude of this designation. One definition of ambassador is the highest ranking person who represents his or her own government while living in another country. That is who we are. We represent, by designation of God, his kingdom here on earth. How do we represent it? *Gospelove!* Through *gospelove* we fulfill the role of ambassador as we bring the message and ministry of reconciliation to this world. An ambassador speaks for the country or kingdom that he represents. He does not speak on his own, but he gives the message of the government that has given him the credentials as ambassador. When we were living in Africa, the United States ambassador to the country we were living in was quoted in the local newspapers as saying some things that were controversial and that were also not totally in line with the US government's policies. He was quickly recalled, which in diplomatic speech means he was fired and replaced.

Jesus uses a similar word for our purpose in Acts 1:8, "But you will receive power when the Holy Spirit comes on you; and you will be my *witnesses* in Jerusalem, and in all Judea and Samaria, and to the ends of the earth." The word *witness* has much the same meaning as *ambassador.* It is a very strong word and is the word from which we derive *martyr.* Jesus is commissioning us in much the same way He did Matthew 28:19-20, "Therefore, go and make disciples of all nations, baptizing them in the name of the Father and the Son and the Holy Spirit, and teaching them to obey everything I have commanded you. And surely I am with you always, to the very end of the age." "Gospel light" does not take these commissions and appointments very seriously. Remember, "Gospel light" is primarily concerned with forgiveness of sins and a ticket to heaven. Everything else seems to be optional. When you look at 2 Corinthians 5:14-20, Acts 1:8, and Matthew 28:19-20, however, you begin to realize that we are saved for something. Our appointment as ambassador is who we are as a new creation in Christ Jesus. It is not just for those we might designate as pastor, evangelist, or missionary.

When I read 2 Corinthians 5:20, "We are therefore Christ's ambassadors, *as though God were making his appeal through us,"* I am confronted with the reality that God has committed this ministry to us, His new creations. It is not so much what I do as who I am. I am a new creation in Christ Jesus and my purpose in this life as a follower of Jesus is to be a part of God's redemptive plan. When you read those words, what comes to your mind? My guess is that many of you, conditioned by years in the church, think in terms of evangelism. I need to witness and present the plan of salvation to people that do not know Christ. We may even feel guilty for a while and make some awkward attempts at trying to communicate the gospel of Jesus. Most of our guilt does not go that far, though, and we give up and rationalize our position by saying that we do not have the gift of evangelism. Actually, the Bible does not specify evangelism as one of the spiritual gifts. Ephesians

4:11 says that Christ gave some people to the church, among them evangelists, but those people are to equip the new creations to do the work of the ministry.

So, how do we do this? How do we live as ambassadors and witnesses to God's redemptive purpose and plan? I have been in and around the church all of my life. I have been called by God and privileged, blessed, and challenged to follow Jesus on this journey called life and ministry. One conclusion that has become clearer and clearer to me is that we make the gospel of Jesus far too complicated. What did Jesus say over and over to his disciples? Follow me and obey my commandments. Ok, so now we begin to make things complicated by trying to parse out the commandments. The Pharisees, the Jewish religious leaders had developed a complicated system of rules based on the ten commandments given through Moses. They had managed to come up with over 500 rules that they were adamant one had to follow to keep the commandments. How many did Jesus have? That's right: **one!** Ok, if you want to be picky, you could say there are two: Love God with all that you are and love your neighbor as yourself. That's it. *Gospelove!* Simple, isn't it? Now, there is a significant difference between *simple* and *easy.* Loving *(gospelove)* God, our neighbor and our enemy is not easy, but it is possible. Jesus would not give us a command and commission and call us His ambassadors, witnesses, and disciples if it were not possible.

Let's look again at Romans 12:1 as expressed in the Message, "Take your everyday ordinary life—your sleeping, eating, going-to-work, and walking around life—and place it before God as an offering." When we read Ephesians 2:10, "For we are God's workmanship, created in Christ Jesus to do good works," we probably begin to think of "good works" as some ministry in the church or through the church. While that might very well be a part, we all have an "everyday, ordinary life, don't we? Whether we realize it or not, God has placed us where we are. Now, many of us have made decisions without consulting God or based upon our own selfish motives, so we should think about that before we blame God for our circumstances or predicaments. Nevertheless, from Psalm 16:5-6 we learn, "Lord, you have assigned me my portion and my cup. The boundary lines have fallen for me in pleasant places." We could spend a long time there, even if we did not consult God in drawing the lines, if we surrender those boundary lines to Him, we will know we are in His place.

I have been in vocational ministry as a pastor, missionary, and denominational leader for over fifty years. One might assume that my life has been lived within the reconciling purpose of God. Even though I have been preaching, teaching, and ministering in the name of, and hopefully, through the power of Jesus Christ, I came to realize that I also had an everyday ordinary life. A major aspect of that everyday life has been my marriage to my wife, LaVonna. I must confess that for many years (too many) I did not think of our marriage in a redemptive context. I wanted the same things most people want in a marriage: love, fulfillment, pleasure, partnership. As long as I thought I was on the receiving end of those things, I was willing to give what I thought was my fair share. As is the case with many couples, what I thought was my fair share and what I thought was my wife's fair share was not necessarily the same as what she thought. Also like many couples, we managed that tension fairly well and, by most accounts, had a solid marriage. Once in a while, though, that tension would surface and we could see that there were some differences. For the most part, we danced around them and managed to avoid any major disasters.

As God began to get my attention and to lead me to become an authentic worshipper, He began to show me His purpose in marriage.

Ephesians 5:25-27 took on a new meaning for me. I had taught and preached on this passage, but now, through the lens of the conviction that Christ died for me helped to no longer look at my wife through my needs and desires. So how was I now to see her? Look at the passage: "Husbands, love (this is *gospelove)* your wives, just as Christ loved the church and gave himself up for her to make her holy, cleansing her by the washing with water through the word, and to present her to himself as a radiant church, without stain or wrinkle or any other blemish, but holy and blameless." Wow, I was stunned. Marriage is not about me and my needs at all. I am to have and demonstrate the same redemptive love that Christ has shown me in dying for me. That led me to give up all the expectations that I had for her. That released a major tension between us and a new freedom and openness began to develop. As we saw in the passage in Philippians 2, it also meant giving up my rights. Now, I know those are fighting words to many, and that is exactly what happens when we feel we have to exercise those rights. One of the biggest of those for me was that I always felt I had to be right, so that in any discussion or argument I would use words and twist things around until I always came out as being right. At least, that's how I saw it. With the ever-present reality of Jesus dying for me and being compelled by His *gospelove*, I began to learn, sometimes painfully, that it is better to be redemptive than to be right.

This did not happen overnight, of course, but God began to remake our marriage to fulfill His purpose. I am to give myself for her and to her to make her holy. That was a completely new dimension of marriage for me. Amazingly enough, when my focus became the redemptive purpose of Christ, many of the things I had sought before in marriage now became by-products of a redemptive relationship. Verse 31 in Ephesians 5 is familiar to many of us, but I was missing where God was leading when He made that statement in Genesis and as it was repeated by Jesus and now Paul. "For this reason a man will leave his father and mother and be united to his wife, and the two will become *one flesh.*" As we live in this covenantal redemptive relationship, God has designed an intimacy for marriage that reflects the relationship He has designed for Christ and His bride, the church.

I began to see other aspects of my everyday ordinary life in the redemptive light of God's purpose, both for me and for the world. One of those is how I spend the money I earn. How redemptive am I in how I use what God has given me? That takes us beyond the issue of tithing and splitting hairs about gross and net income. Our desire over the last few years has been to give more to God and His purpose that we use to live on. We have made significant progress and are blessed to be able to give in a way we never thought would be possible. There are many other areas that look different when we begin to see them in light of our redemptive purpose in Christ. How about our children? How we treat our body? The neighborhood we live in? Our colleagues at work? As you can see, there is really no area of our lives that is outside the realm of our redemptive purpose.

Through the years of our ministry assignments, I have seen a "new" discipleship emphasis rolled out about once per decade. From my perspective, most of those efforts have not been very fruitful. The main reason for this is that we have approached discipleship as a course to study and perhaps follow rather than a lifestyle to be lived out in our everyday ordinary lives. Living out the commandments or *gospelove* should keep us from succumbing to the widespread perception in the church that evangelism and discipleship are separate entities. They are not. Our commission from Jesus in Matthew 28:19-20 to make disciples of all nations makes us realize that discipleship or the process of making disciples begins with the non-believer. We are to *gospelove* our neighbors and enemies and it is through that *gospelove* that the Father draws them to Christ. They are both indispensable elements of the mission and purpose of God: reconciling all of creation unto Himself. We are commissioned to make disciples of all nations. We can only do this through and by the *gospelove* of Christ as we accept the appointment as an ambassador and witness to Him. I have heard often through the ministry journey that the church does not operate in the power of the Holy Spirit as we see in Acts or throughout the history of the church of Jesus Christ. For the most part, I would agree with that. There certainly could be many factors that lead to this lack of power, but it really is all about mission and *gospelove*.

We have approached the power of God back to front. We ask for His power, we pray for His power, we fast for His power, we sing for His power, and then believe that when "the fire falls" that God is going to make everything right and we will see revival, whatever that may look like. According to Matthew 28:18-20, Acts 1:8, 2 Corinthians 5:20, and many other Scriptures, as new creations in Christ, we already have the power and authority of Jesus. We are waiting around for the power when what we need to be doing is obeying the commands of Jesus and His *gospelove.* His power through the Holy Spirit comes as we are obedient (Acts 5:32).

Spiritual gifts, spiritual fruit, and dynamic power are all for one purpose: to do the "good works" God has planned in advance for us. We are to bring our everyday, ordinary, sleeping, eating, going-to-work, walking around life and place it before God as an offering. According to Jesus, his power and authority will be available for whatever we need to accomplish His mission: making disciples through *gospelove.*

MISSION POSSIBLE

They committed themselves to the teaching of the
apostles, the life together, the common meal, and
the prayers. (Acts 2:42, The Message)

Some years ago, LaVonna and I were in the process of buying a house. We went to see a house that was for sale by owner. As they showed us through the house, I noticed a book on the coffee table that I had recently read. It was a Christian book that had the name Jesus in the title. So I asked the owner about the book and he responded that he loved Jesus but he wanted nothing to do with the sick old church. When I told him I was a pastor, there were a few moments of awkward silence that passed between us. I was hoping that he might feel enough embarrassment that he would discount the price of the house, but that did not happen. With the "gospel light" message, the church has also become optional. Consider the following statistics. According to various surveys by those who do such research, 96 per cent of Americans say they believe in God, or a higher power. My first thought is of James 2:19, "You believe there is one God. Good! Even demons believe that—and shudder." Through the same research, 64 per cent of Americans say they have had some kind of "born again" experience. However, only about 25 per cent of Americans regularly attend or are involved in a church. The most common response I hear from someone who proclaims to be a Christian but is not part of a church is, "You don't have to go to church to be a Christian." While this statement may be literally true, it is misleading, to say the least. As a follower of Christ, you do not have to go or be a part of a church, but you will want to. While the evangelical tradition does not hold that salvation is found only in the church, Jesus would strongly express that salvation is to be lived and expressed through and for the church.

Throughout the New Testament, the church is often described as the "body of Christ". Ephesians 5:23 states, "Christ is the head of the church, his body, of which he is the Savior." 1 Corinthians 12:13 says, "For we were all baptized by one Spirit into one body—whether Jews or Greeks, slave or free—and we were all given one Spirit to drink." When we become a new creation in Christ, we are created to be a part of the church of Jesus Christ. When we are baptized, we are baptized into that body, the church. We have seen that in the Old Testament, it is through the nation of Israel that God's covenant with man is realized. In the New Testament, it is through the church that God demonstrates and carries out this covenant. Peter describes this body, the church, in 1 Peter 2:5, "You also, like living stones, are being built into a spiritual house to be a holy priesthood, offering spiritual sacrifices acceptable to God through Jesus Christ." He continues in verse 9, "But you are a chosen people, a royal priesthood, a holy nation, a people belonging to God, that you may declare the praises of him who called you out of darkness into his wonderful light."

When we begin to see through the redemptive lens of what God is doing in the world (2 Corinthians 5:16), we can more clearly see the purpose of the church and our place in that church. When we say that we do not need the church to live as a Christian, we are being self- centered and miss the point for which we were saved. As a new creation in Christ Jesus, we are living from the conviction that Christ died for us and that we "should no longer live for ourselves, but for him who died for us and was raised again." The good works that God has prepared for us (Ephesians 2:10) are to be fulfilled in and through the body of Christ. 1 Corinthians 12:12 says, "The body is a unit, though it is made up of many parts; and though all its parts are many, they form one body." The old axiom that the sum, or whole, is greater than the parts is certainly true of the church. Yes, we all have an everyday ordinary life, but we need to see that as part of God's whole, His redemptive plan. Peter captures this perspective in 1 Peter 3:9, "The Lord is not slow in keeping his promise, as some understand slowness. He is patient with you, not wanting anyone to perish, but everyone to come to repentance."

Our mission was clearly summarized by Jesus in Matthew 28:18-20, "All authority in heaven and on earth has been given to me. Therefore go and make disciples of all nations, baptizing them in the name of the Father and of the Son and of the Holy Spirit, and teaching them to obey everything I have commanded you. And surely I am with you always, to the very end of the age." Think about it! Is there any way we could possibly fulfill Jesus's mission going it alone. If we all do our own thing, saying we do not need each other and we do not need the church, how far do you think we will get in fulfilling the mission of Jesus for His new creations? As a pastor, missionary, denominational leader, and church consultant, I can honestly, heartbreakingly tell you we, the church, are not doing well at all in making disciples of Jesus in the nations. The church does a lot of things, many of them good things, but we do not keep the main thing the main thing. Our churches, rather than being the redemptive body of Christ, have become spiritual consumer centers. Just like the world, we market ourselves. Come and hear our great music. Our preacher is dynamic. Our children and youth programs will make your children want to come to church. We have the best coffee and in addition, you can get free Krispy Kreme doughnuts. When Jesus came into Jerusalem and overturned the tables of the moneychangers at the temple, He did so because the primary focus of the house of God at that time, prayer, had been turned into a market. I think he would do the same thing in our churches today, overturning all of "tables" we have built to satisfy spiritual consumers.

When I responded to the call of God on my life for vocational ministry, I said to Him that I would go anywhere He called me. As I've shared previously, that has led us to Nebraska, Kansas, the

Netherlands, Idaho, back to California, South Africa, Kenya, Rwanda, Congo, and Oregon. Since retiring from denominational leadership, I have served as transition/interim pastor in Utah, Oregon, Modesto, CA, Sapulpa, OK, Falcon, CO, and Paradise, CA. I am well past retirement "age", whatever that is, but the passion and desire for Christ and His church will not seem to "retire". Two different times in our journey we sold everything we had so that we would not be encumbered when we were serving in another country. On each occasion, God graciously and plentifully supplied our needs when we returned home. As I stated before, after living in Congo for a year, the political stability of the country (and Rwanda as well) continued to deteriorate and we moved to Nairobi, Kenya to live. My assignment was still Rwanda and Congo, though for a part of that time, I was also responsible for the beginning of our work in Tanzania. I watched in amazement as Jesus built His church even during the most turbulent economic and political times one could imagine.

On one occasion, LaVonna and I had made a trip to Rwanda and Congo to visit some churches, meet with our leaders, and hopefully bring encouragement to our leaders there. We would spend most of our time in the Goma and Gisenyi area because that is where our leaders were located and where our greatest concentration of churches were located. At that time, there were only two flights per week from Kenya to Rwanda, usually on Tuesday and Friday. We drove from Gisenyi to Kigali, the main city of Rwanda. It was about 100 miles through the beautiful land of a "thousand hills", as it was called. We would try and make this drive on Thursday so we could go by the office of Kenya Airways to see if there was going to be a flight to Nairobi the next day and to confirm that we were still listed as passengers. So on this particular Thursday, we left Gisenyi in the early afternoon. While the road was one of the best in that part of Africa, there were obstacles. Guerilla warfare had been taking place in Rwanda for the past few years and that meant that there would be military roadblocks along the highway. Depending on the situation, there could be anywhere from five to twenty-five stops along the one hundred mile route.

On this particular day, there were about five or six stops. When you stopped, soldiers with military rifles would check you car, open the trunk, ask you a few questions, and check your papers, passports, etc. Sometimes a soldier would ask if they could ride with you to Kigali. When they leaned in the window with that rifle on their shoulder, it did not seem prudent to say no. On this day, at the second stop, we had two soldiers ask for a ride. We obliged and it actually helped us because at the remaining stops, they would wave us through when they saw the soldiers in the back seat. Kigali is a city of hills, and as we came into the city, we were on the lower plane. At the first stop, we saw broken glass and rocks in the road, which was unusual. As we started up the hill toward the center of town, there were some young men running down the road with rocks in their hands, yelling something, and looking as if they were going to throw rocks at our car. When they saw the soldiers in the backseat, they waved us through and gave us no trouble. As we reached the center of town, the soldiers asked us to let them out and we went on the the missionary guest house where we were staying that night. We decided not to try and go by the Kenya Airways office because there were crowds all along the roads and it did not look too safe to be on the road. When we reached the guest house, we asked the lady in charge what had been happening. She related that there were political riots all day long and some business places had been attacked, looted, and even burned. We were thankful we did not have to go anywhere that evening and hoped and prayed there would be calm in the city the next day.

The next morning, we left the guest house and went downtown to turn in our rental car and be taken to the airport. From what we could see, it appeared that the riots were over and people were about their business. However, we did come upon a police roadblock and they said there was a detour and we should take another route downtown. We finally arrived at the office, turned in our car, and had a driver who would take us to the airport. The airport was located at the edge of the city, about five or more miles from where we were. As we were coming out of the office parking lot onto the main street, we heard a loud noise and looked up. There was a mob of people running up the street, yelling, throwing rocks, and many of them yielding sticks like weapons. As we were watching this take place, we did not realize that our car was surrounded by a number of men. They started yelling at the driver and banging on the car top and windows. I was yelling at our driver to go, but he seemed to be paralyzed by fear. The men began to rock our car and I knew then what was coming. They would bounce it until they could flip it over and then set it on fire. One of the men looked at me through the passenger window and I thought I could see in his eyes that he was saying this was not our fight, but we were caught in it nevertheless. I turned to LaVonna, who was sitting in the backseat, took her hand and said, "I guess this is it." At that moment, in the midst of this life-threatening frenzy and chaos, I felt a peace from the Lord. Yes, I was frightened, particularly about what might happen to LaVonna, but we both had a peace.

Suddenly, just at the moment when they were ready to flip the car, for no apparent reason they walked away. When I saw the opening, I yelled at the driver to go and he finally got us moving. As we drove to the airport, we saw crowds of people and were not sure if we would be stopped or caught. Finally, though, we reached the airport. When LaVonna and I stepped out of the car, our knees buckled and we could hardly walk. The plane finally arrived, we boarded and flew back to Nairobi. We did not see anyone from our mission that day or Saturday. The more we reflected on those moments, the more surreal they seemed to become. On Sunday morning, one of our volunteer missionaries saw LaVonna and exclaimed how happy she was to see us. She had been listening to BBC radio and heard of the riots in Kigali. She knew we were there and were returning on Friday and she said that she had been in prayer for us all that day. I knew, then, why those men just walked away from the car. As I have reflected on that incident through the years since, I know that God spared us that day. Only He fully knows the how and why, but I know that I am still here for a reason, and that reason is Jesus.

If someone asks you today, whether you are a new creation in Christ or not, "Who is Jesus Christ?", what would you say. In Matthew 16, we see Jesus and His disciples taking some moments of reflection. The disciples had seen Jesus do some amazing, inexplicable things and they were trying to process it all. Then, in verse 13, Jesus asks the disciples, "Who do people say the Son of Man is?" They give various responses that include John the Baptist, Elijah, Jeremiah, or one of the prophets. Then Jesus zeroes in by asking, "But what about you? Who do you say I am?" Peter answers, "You are the Christ, the Son of the living God." Jesus responds in verse 18 by saying, "Blessed are you, son of Jonah. . .And I tell you that you are Peter, and on this rock I will build my church." Then, a few sentences later, Jesus explains what it means for each follower for Jesus to build His church. Verse 24 says, "If anyone would come after me, he must deny himself and take up his cross and follow me. For whoever wants to save his life will lose it, but whoever loses his life for me will find it." Not exactly "gospel light", is it?

What does it mean for one to "take up his cross"? A simple explanation is for us take the "good works" described in Ephesians 2:10 and fulfill the everyday purpose God has for our lives. To "take up his cross" means that we are compelled by the redemptive love of Jesus (2 Corinthians 5:14) and that we are living from the conviction that Jesus died for us. It means that we have recognized and accepted the appointment as Christ's *ambassador,* as though God makes His appeal through us (2 Corinthians 5:20). Why do we have to deny ourselves? Before we were new creations in Christ, we lived for our own desires, dreams, pleasures, and goals. Now, we see life differently. It is not about us! It is about Jesus and what He is doing in the world. So how do we live this out? We can discover an amazing blueprint in Acts 2, as the church of Jesus Christ is born and begins to make a redemptive impact on the world.

Being involved in the church all of my life, I am continually surprised when I look at the beginning of the church. We have often analyzed the church to the point that we have perhaps made the church some things it was not meant to be. It is interesting that Jesus did not give His disciples much instruction about how the church was to be organized, how the liturgy was supposed to be expressed, how many elders and deacons there should be, and what the exact duties of the pastor should be. His main focus was to wait for the power of the Holy Spirit. He describes the grand redemptive plan in Acts 1:8, "But you will receive power when the Holy Spirit comes on you; and you will be my witnesses in Jerusalem, and in all Judea and Samaria, and to the ends of the earth." I do not think the disciples knew exactly what they were waiting for, and I am fairly certain they had no plan or even concept of what it meant to reach to the ends of the earth. So how did it happen?

On the day of the feast of Pentecost, which was one of the major Jewish feasts of the year, they were together in Jerusalem and the Holy Spirit came upon them. It was rather messy and noisy, according to Acts 2:1-3. Then, verse 4 states that they (approximately 120) "were filled with the Holy Spirit". Others heard the noise and commotion and wondered what was happening. Peter then stood before the crowds and delivered the first sermon recorded in the church. He basically gave testimony to who Jesus was, what He did in His death and resurrection, and that He was now exalted at the right hand of God. The conviction of the Holy Spirit came upon the crowd and they asked Peter what they should do. Peter responded in Acts 2:38, "Repent and be baptized, every one of you, in the name of Jesus Christ for the forgiveness of your sins. And you will receive the gift of the Holy Spirit. The promise is for you and your children and for all who are far off—for all whom the Lord our God will call." What happened next is truly amazing and extraordinary as described in verse 41, "Those who accepted his message were baptized, and about three thousand were added to their number that day." Really? Are you serious? The church is not even one day old and they already have three thousand people. What do they do now?

I am not sure how many days, weeks, or months might have passed between verse 41 and verse 42, but we do see how this new, rapidly growing church functioned. Let us look at verses 42-47: "They devoted themselves to the apostles' teaching and to fellowship, to the breaking of bread and to prayer. Everyone was filled with awe at the many wonders and signs performed by the apostles. All the believers were together and had everything in common. They sold property and possessions to give to anyone who had need. Every day they continued to meet together in the temple courts. They broke bread in their homes and ate together with glad and sincere hearts, praising God and enjoying the favor of all the people. And the Lord added to their number daily those who were being saved." Now, we have to ask ourselves if that description of the life of this new church has much or any semblance of what we know as the church in the twenty-first century? The obvious response is a resounding "No!" Of course, there are many theologians and church leaders who have many explanations of why the church looks so different today than it did in the book of Acts. Life is different. The world is different. So, the church is different. That is not surprising, but the major question needs to be is the church fulfilling the purpose for which it was created? In the Matthew 16 passage, Jesus responded to Peter's declaration that Jesus is "the Christ, the Son of the living God" by saying "Blessed are you Simon son of Jonah, for this was not revealed to you by flesh and blood, but by my father in heaven. And I tell you that you are Peter, and on this rock *I will build my church.*" (Matthew 16:17-18)

As I continued in the journey of ministry, I became aware of the fact that I should be building the church. I was told this by college professors, seminary professors, denominational leaders, and pastoral colleagues. Of course, Jesus would help me, but primarily it was up to me. When I would begin to read in Scripture of the church and think that perhaps we were not on the right track or moving in the right direction, I was reassured by the leaders mentioned above that I just needed to do the things we had done in the past by trying harder, being more consistent, and keeping at it and we would see results. Some of that was true, of course. I began to sense, however, that the "results" I was seeing were not necessarily the "results" Jesus was talking about. Through the years, I became more and more aware of what I felt was a major issue in the church: the issue of wineskins. Let us look at Jesus and see what we can discover.

In the gospel of Luke, chapter five, verse 33 we read of a very interesting, though somewhat obscure conversation Jesus had with the religious leaders of his day. "One day some people said to Jesus, 'John the Baptist's disciples fast and pray regularly, and so do the disciples of the Pharisees. Why are your disciples always eating and drinking?' Jesus responded, 'Do wedding guests fast while celebrating with the groom? Of course not. But some day the groom will be taken away from them, and then they will fast.'" Then Jesus gave them this illustration: 'No one tears a piece of cloth from a new garment and uses it to patch an old garment. For them the new garment would be ruined, and the new patch wouldn't even match the old garment. And no one puts new wine into old wineskins. For the new wine would burst the wineskins, spilling the wine and ruining the skins. New wine must be stored in new wineskins. But no one who drinks the old wine seems to want the new wine. The old wine is just fine, they say." (Luke 5:33-38, NLT)

You do not have to read very far into one of the gospels, Matthew, Mark, Luke, or John to realize that Jesus was constantly at odds with the leaders of the Jewish religion. Usually these are named Pharisees and Sadducees. While it is not always named as such, the issue was usually the wine and the wineskins. Jesus was bringing a new message and kingdom lifestyle. He started well as recorded in Luke 4:16. "When he came to the village in Nazareth, his boyhood home, he went as usual to the synagogue on the Sabbath and stood up to read the Scriptures. The scroll of the prophet was handed to him. He unrolled the scroll and found the place where this was written: 'The Spirit of the Lord is upon me, for he has anointed me to bring Good News to the poor. He has sent me to proclaim that captives will be released, that the blind will see, that the oppressed will be set free, and that the time of the Lord's favor has come.'

He rolled up the scroll, handed it back to the attendant and sat down." So far, so good. Hey, this guy is on the same page; we all read Isaiah as it is part or our tradition. But Jesus did not stop there. Verse 21 describes what happened next; "Then he (Jesus) began to speak to them. 'The Scriptures you've just heard has been fulfilled this very day.' " Really, Jesus? Couldn't you have taken it a bit slower? However, from that day on the relationship between Jesus and the religious leaders was contentious, to say the least. Why? When Jesus said that the Scriptures had been filled this very day, he was presenting himself as the new wine of the revelation of God the

Father. This is what John is describing in his gospel, chapter one, verse eleven, "He came to his own people, and even they rejected him." Jesus was the new wine of the new covenant, but they were not ready for him. I am sure many of us mentally scold or even castigate the Jewish leaders and people of the day for not recognizing Jesus for he was (the Messiah) and the covenant/kingdom lifestyle he was bringing. Before we do, however, we need to see how comfortable we are with the old wineskins.

When I was a young pastor, I was trying to teach the leaders of the church where I was pastor how to reach people through personal evangelism. A good group had responded to follow me to learn how we could take the gospel message outside the church walls and present Jesus to people that were not likely to come into the church. This particular week, we watched a video presentation of someone who presented the gospel in a home and the person to whom it was being presented repented and prayed to receive Christ as Savior. After the video, one of the leaders said he just could not believe that a person could be "born again" if he did not come to the church, kneel at the altar and repent in front of those who were there to pray for him. This was the wineskin he had known all of his life in the church and he could not receive the "new wine" of someone receiving Christ outside the church walls.

So, the issues of Jesus healing or picking grain on the Sabbath, eating or drinking with "sinners", talking to women of dubious reputation, teaching the disciples how to pray, eating "unclean" food were all wineskin issues. The old wineskins could not hold the "new wine" of the message and lifestyle of Jesus. Jesus is quite clear that the new wine must be stored in new wineskins. I am convinced that the church of today has a wineskin problem. God, in His grace, is constantly revealing himself to us in new ways. He is an infinite

91

God, so there is no end to the ways in which He reveals himself to us through the Holy Spirit living in us.

One of my favorite descriptions of this new wine is described in the conversation Jesus had with one of these leaders in John 3. "Now there was a Pharisee, a man named Nicodemus who was a member of the Jewish ruling council. He came to Jesus at night and said, 'Rabbi, we know you are a teacher who has come from God. For no one could perform the signs you are doing if God were not with him.' Jesus replied, 'Very truly I tell you, no one can enter the kingdom of God unless they are born of water and the Spirit. Flesh gives birth to flesh, but the Spirit gives birth to spirit. You should not be surprised at my saying, 'You must be born again.' The wind blows wherever it pleases. You hear its sound, but you cannot tell where it comes from or where it is going. So it is with everyone born of the Spirit.' " (John 3:1-8) As we have seen throughout this book, Jesus describes the new wine of becoming a new creation in Christ Jesus (2 Corinthians 5:17). We are born of the Spirit and the new wine of the life of Christ lives within us. While in this passage he describes this life by a description of the wind, in another place it is described as "rivers of living waters" that will flow from within us. (John 7:38) We often start this way in the new life in Christ, but as we are consistently exposed to the wineskins of the church, we do not experience the life, the power, the freshness that the seems to be the focus of Jesus. Think about the wind. Jesus says that we hear its sound, but we cannot tell where it comes from or where it is going. For most of us, that is scary so we seek something more sensible. Let's face it; the wind leaves a mess.

Look what happened when the new wine of the Spirit came on the day of Pentecost. "When the day of Pentecost came, they were all together in one place. Suddenly a sound like the blowing of a violent wind came from heaven and filled the whole house where they were sitting. They saw what seemed to be tongues of fire that separated and came to rest on each of them. All of them were filled with the Holy Spirit and began to speak in other tongues as the Spirit enabled them. Now there were staying in Jerusalem God-fearing Jews from every nation under heaven. When they heard this sound, a crowd came together in bewilderment, because each one hears their own language being spoken. Utterly amazed, they asked: 'Aren't all these who are speaking Galileans? Then how is it that each of us hears them in our native language?

Parthians, Medes and Elamites; residents of Mesopotamia, Judea and Cappadocia, Pontus and Asia, Phyrgia and Pamphylia, Egypt and the parts of Libya near Cyrene; visitors from Rome (both Jews and converts to Judaism); Cretans and Arabs—we hear them declaring the wonders of God in our own tongues!' Amazed and perplexed, they asked one another, 'What does this mean?'

"Some, however, made fun of them and said, 'They have had too much wine,' " They had, of course, had a lot of wine, but not the kind you drink. They were full of the new wine of Jesus the Christ through the Holy Spirit. And it was a mess. Can you imagine three thousand people being baptized and added to the church in one day? What do you do with that? There were no wineskins for that event. Throughout the book of Acts, there are wineskins forming around the wine of the Spirit as the wind continues to blow. In some cases, the old wineskins had to be faced and put aside. When I use the term "wineskin", it is basically how we do church and how we live out the life of Jesus in us. Let us look at some of our present wineskins and how we arrived at how and perhaps even why we do church. Then we can ask the question if these present wineskins can hold the new wine God continues to pour out through the Holy Spirit.

I want us to look again at verse 39 in Luke chapter 5. Jesus says, "But no one who drinks the old wine seems to want the new wine. 'The old is just fine,' they say". (NLT) I am convinced this is where the church, particularly in the USA, is living. Most of my ministry I have been told by leaders to just try harder and do things better. I have heard so many calls for that "old time religion" and a good old fashioned revival that I could not count them. Do you realize that old time religion and good old fashioned revival are wineskins in and of themselves. We want revival to come, but only if it is what we are looking for. Meanwhile, the wind is blowing and we are ducking for cover, behind the secure walls of the church that longs for the old does not want to taste or experience the new.

In the fifth chapter of Matthew, Jesus begins to reveal to his followers what it means to follow him and experience his kingdom on earth. In 5:13 he says, "You are the salt of the earth. But if the salt loses its saltiness, how can it be made salty again? It is no longer good for anything, except to be thrown out and trampled underfoot. You are the light of the world. A town built on a hill cannot be hidden. Neither do people light a lamp and put it under a bowl. Instead they put it on its stand, and it gives light to everyone in the house. In the same way, let your light shine before others, that they may see your good deeds and glorify your Father in heaven." (Matthew 5:13-16) Verse 13 in The Message reads as follows, "Let me tell you why you are here. You're here to be salt-seasoning that brings out the God-flavors of this earth. If you lose your saltiness, how will people taste godliness?"

There was a time, even a long period of time in America, when the church influenced the culture and brought out the "God flavors of this earth." Let us look at the century from 1870 to 1970. Those dates can be arbitrary, but I believe they illustrate the change in the church and the culture. For that century, the salt of the church was reflected in the moral values of the culture at large. For those one hundred years, the culture gave the church the day of Sunday. It is interesting to note the progression of how Sunday was perceived through the generations of that century. First Sunday was referred to as the Holy Sabbath, then the Sabbath, then the Lord's Day, then Sunday, then the weekend. For most of that time, the culture left Sunday alone and gave it to the church. Stores, movie theaters, bowling alleys, skating rinks, and most other entertainment or shopping venues, even bars, were all closed on Sunday.

The church took advantage of the day almost all of the disciple making activities took place on Sunday. My dad was born in 1915 and he told me that in the 1920's and 1930's that if a church had anything going on a Sunday night, they were literally the only show in town. So, Sunday night became a time of evangelism when the unchurched or those who had left the church would come because there was nothing else to do. As a result, many people would respond to an evangelistic appeal and come to Christ. Sunday night evangelism became a wineskin. I entered the ministry in 1970 and one of the first books given to me by a leader in our denomination was something like, "The Church Winning Evangelism on Sunday Nights". Now, the Sunday night effective evangelism ship had sailed over twenty-five years before, but we kept beating that drum for fifty years. By 1970, the people who came to Sunday night service were the most faithful from Sunday morning, usually less than half the congregation. We kept up the mantra of do it more and do it better and we continued to get people saved over and over again. The Sunday night wineskin was old and could not hold the new wine, though the infinite God was sending it, as He always does.

As I grew up during the 1950's and 1960's, I am thankful to God that I had Christian parents who believed that we should be in church when there was a service. As a result, we would spend three to five hours in church every Sunday. We would begin with Sunday School around 9:30 A.M. and have an age group Bible lesson. Even though the churches we attended were usually small, we always had age group classes. After an hour or an hour and fifteen minutes, we would attend the morning worship service. There we would sing and pray together and the pastor would give a Bible based sermon. We would also observe the sacraments of communion and baptism, though not often. Then we would return in the late afternoon for a children or youth meeting followed by the evening worship service. The only regular church activity we had that was not on Sunday would be the Wednesday evening prayer service. So, as a child and teen growing up in the church I was discipled primarily on Sunday. As a family we would attend probably 50 Sundays of the year.

As the church grew and developed, we used our resources and energy for what took place on Sunday. We built buildings that we called sanctuaries and they were only used for perhaps three hours on Sunday. We could not eat or drink or run or play in these sanctuaries, so we had to build other buildings in which to have "fellowship", but they were also mostly used on Sundays. As the church moved to the suburbs, we built expansive parking lots that again were only used on Sunday. As staff began to be added to help the pastor, it was mostly "Sunday" staff; children's church leaders, youth leaders, and worship/music leaders. We began to measure the health or viability of the church by what took place on Sunday. How many people came, how much money did they bring, how many were saved or born again, how many became members. And for many of those years, the measurement of the Sunday model was a good indicator of the the health of the church as disciples were being made in this model.

By 1980, though, the sanctity of Sunday in the culture had not only broken down, but had been totally flipped upside down. Sunday now became the culture's day for the best of everything, from sports to entertainment to shopping to all kinds of activities. When the three day weekend came along, we knew were going to have at least one Sunday every month of low attendance because of the three day weekend. School used to start the week after Labor Day in most places. It would seem to me that one of the lowest attended Sundays of the year was Labor Day, as people would take one last trip before school started. I mentioned that as I grew up my family was in church for three to five hours for fifty or more Sundays a year. Now the leaders and most faithful members of a congregation are in church for an hour and fifteen minutes a week and are present for an average of thirty to thirty two weeks a year. While we continually call for a greater commitment from the people in the church, we are not going to get Sundays back. To make disciples, which is the mission of the church as commissioned by Jesus (Matthew 28-19-20), we are going to have to provide other avenues of teaching and ministry. Many, if not most, churches are trying to do that. We provide classes, small groups, and many different types of ministry, whether within the walls of the church or out in the community. However, the main focus is still the Sunday model. Most of our resources, people, and energy are directed to the Sunday or weekend service.

Even though the reality has changed, the measurement has not. Wherever you look for statistics regarding the church, you will find that the church in the USA is not only static, but in decline. There are many factors that are involved in such a statement, but one I rarely (if ever) hear about is that the model of one church, one pastor, one building is no longer viable either economically or spiritually or missional. The average sized congregation of a protestant church congregation in the USA is less than 100 congregants. In the economic reality that we presently live in, how can a church with 75-90 people support a pastor, a building facility, and try and develop ministries in the community? Economically, this model is no longer viable. However, it is not just economically viable, but missional as well.

For the past one hundred fifty years, as the Sunday model wineskins were developed, the church has been saying to the world around them, "Come and join us." We are encouraged by our pastors to invite our neighbors and friends to church. Nothing wrong with that and we should do it as often as we can. It is, though, the wineskin of come and see us and engage us on our level that needs to be changed and is no longer effective. We now live in a post Christian, secular culture, as difficult as that may be for those of us in the church to admit and comprehend. In that culture, people are no longer going to turn to the church when they hit bumps in the road or even major catastrophes and tragic situations. The church is simply not on their radar. More and more, if secular people, probably about 60 per cent of the population, depending on where you live, even know of the church, they see it from a political perspective. The culture has little or no connection to any church and if they did come and engage us where we are, they would have little or no understanding of what we are or what we are doing. Our traditions, language, and rituals would be foreign to them. That does not mean that traditions and rituals are meaningless; simply that a secular world is on a different level. So, if that is the case, what do we do? We need a new wineskin that will engage the culture on their level.

A LIFE WORTH LIVING

We have seen through the Word of God that every person who becomes a "new creation in Christ" and is "born of the Spirit" has a purpose in life (Ephesians 2:10). We continue to live our every day, ordinary life but now there is meaning and purpose in being a part of something that is absolutely life changing and world changing. So, how would you like to change the world? That is what God has planned and He has invited us to be a part of His reconciling, redemptive process that will lead ultimately to "a new heaven and a new earth, where righteousness dwells." (2 Peter 3:13) He has appointed us ambassadors of this new kingdom and He has empowered us to be His "witnesses". If that is true and truly what God has planned, why do we not see more fruit in the churches across our land and world? Why is the church in decline, both in impact in the culture and in participation by the people?

That is perhaps a complex question and you can find many explanations that would add considerably to that complexity. However, if we stick to Jesus and His Word, there really is nothing complex about it. We simply have to be focused and obedient to what Jesus has commanded and commissioned us to do. Over and over during His earthly journey, Jesus says simply that if we love Him, we will obey His commandments. He then makes His commandment clear as recorded in Mark 12:29-31, "The most important one (commandment)," answered Jesus, "is this: 'Hear, O Israel: The Lord our God is one. Love the Lord your God with all your heart and with all your soul and with all your mind and with all your strength.' The second is this: 'Love your neighbor as yourself.' There is no commandment greater than these." *Gospelove,* which we have defined and explained throughout this book. That is really all we have to do to follow Jesus. Simple, right? Remember, there is a difference between *simple* and *easy.* To show and do *gospelove* to our neighbors and our enemies is not necessarily easy. It is, though, indispensable for God's redemptive plan and process.

In His instructions to His disciples, Jesus said clearly that "I will build my church" (Matthew 16:18). What are we to do? He gives us one commission, "All authority in heaven and on earth has been given to me. Therefore go and make disciples of all nations, baptizing them in the name of the Father and of the Son and of the Holy Spirit, and teaching them to obey everything I have commanded you. And surely I am with you always , to the very end of the age." (Matthew 28:18-20) Simple, right? That is a clear commission from the cornerstone, capstone, and head of the body of Christ, the church. So, why do we not see the church thriving and the number of disciples growing? **We simply do not believe that Jesus meant what He said!** That is a bold statement. The Bible clearly defines faith and belief as action words. We do what we believe and and we believe what we do, paraphrasing James 2:18. The mission statement of the denomination I have been a part of my entire life has as its mission statement: To make Christlike disciples in the nations. Perfect; exactly what Jesus said we should be about. There is only one big problem: **We don't believe it!** As a pastor and later as a district superintendent I have been required to submit many different reports about the church and what we did in a particular year or period of time. Through multiple pages I would report on my own spiritual condition, how many people did I call on in their homes, how many sermons did I preach, how many people came to our services each week, how much money did they bring with them, what was the value of our buildings and facility, how many were in each age group, nursery, pre-school, elementary, teens, young adults, middle aged adults, senior adults, and that is just a partial list. Through fifty-five years of ministry, I never had to answer a single question about making disciples. **Not one!** The one thing that Jesus commissions us to do and we do not do it. Our wineskins have no place where that fits. Oh, leaders have said that all of these things that we report are a part of making disciples. Perhaps they are, but when I was District Superintendent I asked pastors and church boards directly if they had a process of making disciples and some way to measure how we were doing. Guess what? They didn't. They hoped disciples were being made through some or all of their ministries, but they were not intentional about it. I really think Jesus was intentional, don't you?

What would happen if our focus was in line with what the writer of the book of Hebrews said, "And let us run with perseverance the race marked out for us, fixing our eyes (focus) on Jesus, the pioneer and perfecter of our faith. For the joy set before him he endured the cross, scorning its shame, and sat down at the right hand of God." (Hebrews 12:1-3) If our focus is really on Jesus we will hear His priorities, commandments, and commission. Love God. Love our neighbor. Love our enemy. Make disciples. In John 6:44 Jesus says, "No one can come to me unless the Father who sent me draws them." Later in the same chapter He says, "This is why I told you that no one can come to me unless the Father has enabled them." (verse 65) How, then, does the Father draw people to Christ? One of the ways, perhaps the primary way, is that we obey the commands of Jesus to *gospelove* our neighbor and enemy. It is amazing to me that God would use us in this great redemption, but He does. When he appoints us as ambassador, Paul states that it is "as though God were making his appeal through us." Many of us who have been in and around the church automatically think of some kind of "gospel presentation" as an appeal. It may be, but the appeal comes through our life of *gospelove* which gives the Holy Spirit right of way to draw people to Jesus. How do we simplify this without making it some kind of "program" or "ministry" that usually ends up being for a few "qualified" people. No, this is for all who believe, who are new creations in Christ Jesus, who have been "born of the Spirit" and who are focused on following Jesus. Is that you? Then, let's go and change the world.

In Matthew chapter 13 Jesus tells us the parable of the sower. I have heard and read of various interpretations of this parable and its meaning. I would like for us to keep it as simple and directive as possible as I believe we can find a focused direction of being followers of Jesus. So, we pick up the story in verse 3, "A farmer went out to sow his seed. As he was scattering the seed, some fell along the path, and the birds came and ate it up. Some fell on rocky places, where it did not have much soil. It sprang up quickly, because the soil was shallow. But when the sun came up, the plants were scorched, and they withered because they had no root. Other seed fell among the thorns, which grew up and choked the plants. Still other seed fell on good soil, where it produced a crop—a hundred, sixty, or thirty times what was sown. Whoever has ears, let them hear." (Matthew 13:3-9) When you read that brief description of the sower, what stands out to you? If you have heard sermons or teaching on the parable, they might have influenced your thinking. First, let us try and see the context. A farmer went out. Where did he go? To the synagogue; to the temple? No, he went out to or toward the fields, which is where you would expect a farmer to go. He is going about his everyday, ordinary life. This parable is recorded also in the gospel of Luke and the gospel of Mark. In each case the seed is the word of God or the message of the kingdom. Now, let's pause here and think for a moment. The wineskin we have developed over the centuries in the church is for a pastor to sow the seed, the message, the Word of God. If that were to be the message of Jesus, though, do you not think He would have used a rabbi, priest, or religious leader who would have been sowing the seed? When we read the parable through that wineskin, we then see the different types of soil as indicative of the church, or in Jesus' day, the synagogue or the temple. If the soil in the church is good, we can expect a harvest. I have heard many times (way too many) pastors declaring that their church is "reaching in so we can reach out." Sounds good, doesn't it? It is not good and it *never* happens that way.

What is the message of the seed, then? *Gospelove!* We are to be *gospeloving* our God, our neighbor, and our enemy. The message may be in the form of a cup of cold water, a helping hand, a kind word or deed, or expressed in many other ways. The farmer was intentional; "he went out to sow seed". He had a purpose in what he was doing. What was that purpose? The **harvest.** When we are *intentional* and *proactive* in *gospeloving* our neighbor and our enemy, God the Father draws people to Jesus and that is the harvest. *Proactive* means that we take the initiative whether or not they give an opening or respond to something we say or do. The farmer continued to sow seed. To think *intentional* and *proactive,* look with me at Romans 5:8, "But God demonstrates his own love for us in this: While we were still sinners, Christ died for us." That is how we are to share the *gospelove* to our world. Now, again the question: What do you see when you read the description in the parable? Do we ever see the crop, the harvest? One hundred times what was sown. Many teachings think that the use of numbers by Jesus was just a throwaway, even hyperbole. Well, He said the same thing in all three recordings that we have and He uses the same numbers. Why would we think that an exponential crop would be beyond the scope of God? Remember what Peter wrote in 2 Peter 3:9, "The Lord is not slow in keeping his promise, as some understand slowness. Instead he is patient with you, not wanting any to perish, but everyone to come to repentance." Remember Peter's own experience with an exponential harvest. Before he was Peter, the rock, he was Simon, the fisherman. When Jesus first called him, he was using Peter's boat as a sort of podium at the edge of the lake. Then he told Peter to "Put out into deep waters, and let down the nets for a catch." (Matthew 5:4) Peter reluctantly did what Jesus asked and the result was "they caught such a large number of fish that their nets began to break." It happened again to Peter in John 21; a "miraculous" catch. Frankly, we in the church do not really want to see this kind of harvest as it is too hard to control and it will not fit into the current wineskins that we have developed.

One church where I was the pastor we actually experienced, if not exponential, at least explosive growth. A few times I was asked by another church or conference to share our experience; how did you do it? I was such a disappointment that people stopped asking me to come. They wanted a formula, three easy steps to build their church. My first point was always that our experience was really a God thing and that Jesus said that He would build His church. We took Him at His word and stopped trying to build the church. Now that was against everything I had been taught in college, seminary, and from church leaders. We began to ask ourselves what are we doing or not doing that is keeping Jesus from building His church? That is not what people wanted to hear, so they crossed me from their list. Do we believe Jesus said what He meant and meant what He said in the parable of the sower? If we are faithful to sow the seeds of the *gospelove* will the Father draw more and more people to the Christ, the Son of the living God? He says He will and I believe Him. When we read the interpretation of the parable, given by Jesus, by the way, we can get distracted. When I have asked people to identify their *neighbor* so they could begin praying and looking for ways to demonstrate *gospelove* to them, I watch them go through a process. They usually eliminate people from their consideration by saying they will never be interested in God, the gospel, or the church. I believe the interpretation of the parable can be instructive for us at this point.

We could rightly ask why a farmer, who should know what he is doing, sow seeds on the hard path, or the rocky soil, or among the thorns? Listen to what Jesus says about the hard soil, "When anyone hears the message about the kingdom and does not understand it, the evil one comes and snatches away what was sown in their heart." Our culture has now become a post Christian, secular culture, so the people do not understand the gospel in the way they did fifty years ago. The clear message, though, is that we must continue to sow the seeds of *gospelove* even if we think they do not care, are not interested, or antagonistic. The love of God comes in an unlimited supply, so we never run short and we must leave the harvest to God. Remember what the Word says in the last verse of Acts chapter 2 when describing the development of the beginning days of the church, "And the Lord added to their number daily those who were being saved." (Acts 2:47) There are many who look at statements like that and say that was for the beginning, but it is different today. Well, it is different, but I do not think that is because it has to be. When we received our assignment to go to Rwanda and Congo, I was the pioneer missionary for our denomination. I have mentioned the leaders that God had provided and I watched in awe as Jesus built His church in a way that I had never seen, but certainly resembled more of the book of Acts than the church I grew up in the USA. However, if we sow the seeds of *gospelove* faithfully, intentionally, and proactively, God will do what He loves to do, draw people to Jesus. In the church where we experienced explosive growth, we had a large worship choir. It was not the traditional, robed choir who would sing anthems (nothing wrong with those) but it was a large worship group and my wife and I enjoyed singing in that group for many years. As Jesus was building His church and the people were sharing *gospelove,* I would sometimes hear one of the choir group members say, "Oh, I just saw (name) come in the worship center. They are the last person I thought I would ever see in church." My heart would leap each time I heard that and remind me that God was doing things beyond our own capabilities.

In verses 20-21 Jesus says, "the seed falling on rocky ground refers to someone who hears the word and at once receives it with joy. But since they have no root, they last only a short time. When trouble or persecution comes because of the word, they quickly fall away." This is a definition of the "gospel light" we have been talking about throughout this book. Remember the survey we sighted that said that

64 per cent of all Americans have had some kind of "born again" experience? As our evangelism developed in the twentieth century toward mass evangelism and then what I would call "confrontational" evangelism, our appeal to many was to repent of your sins, accept Jesus as Savior, and receive eternal life. Now, that is all in accord with what we find in the New Testament, but that is not all. In what I feel is our eagerness to spread the gospel, we have created a belief system that does not really fulfill the commandments and commissions of Jesus. Following Jesus and becoming His disciple and being involved in His church and His mission are all options, but what really matters to many is that we said the sinner's prayer and we have a ticket to heaven. There are many doctrinal expressions at this point, and unfortunately we spend more time debating those than we do fulfilling the mission and calling of Jesus. I have been a part of a denomination all of my life and ministry and when I am asked to explain what we believe or where we stand with other groups we always begin with our differences. We believe this or that about eternal security, speaking in tongues, how we do baptism, the role of the Holy Spirit, etc. We always point to the differences. Rarely do we ever come together and exalt the person and name of Jesus. So, the thing to do is to be part of a non-denominational church, right? Sorry, but there is no such thing. Every church, independent or non-denominational or whatever you may want to call it, has their wineskins of how they do church. It may be written or unwritten, but it is "how we do things around here".

What I want us to see about the "rocky ground" is that Jesus still sows seeds there. He does not go off and try and find ground that is soft with no rocks, weeds, or thorns. No, he continues to sow seed wherever He goes, which is what we are to do in our everyday, ordinary life. We do not give up sowing seeds just because the ground or soil does not seem receptive to growing a harvest. Let's look at verse 22, "The seed falling among the thorns refers to someone who hears the word, but the worries of this life and the deceitfulness of wealth chokes the word, making it unfruitful." He mentions a "hard path" and "rocky ground" but when He comes to the "thorns", He identifies the thorns and defines them specifically: "the worries of this life and the deceitfulness of wealth". Sounds like an apt description of the American culture, does it not? Again, this can be a result of the "gospel light" approach, which really is more man-centered and focused than Christ-centered. We want our cake, forgiveness of sins and a place in heaven, but we want to eat it, too. We continue to live more of a lifestyle of "we only go around once, so grab all we can get." Jesus speaks to these "worries of this life" directly in Matthew 6:25-34 and shows us the way through them in verse 33, "But seek first his kingdom and his righteousness, and all of these things will be given to you as well." The deceitfulness of wealth is well- chronicled throughout Scripture, but most of us believe those admonitions, warnings, and punishments are for someone else, not us. We have no problem with money, as long as we can just get a little more. Remember the word, "deceitful". For those of us who are focused and committed to follow the command and commission of Jesus to sow the seeds of *gospelove,* the message is the same for the hard or rocky ground: **keep sowing seeds!** Remember, God is using us to show *gospelove* to people as His ambassador and His witness. He will bring forth the harvest as He draws people to Jesus through our obedience of love and faithfulness.

Whether you are a believer or follower of Jesus or not, you have some impression or image of God and/or Jesus and who they are. Maybe you grew up in a church and "rebelled" at some point or maybe things just did not make sense or maybe you have never even thought of God as a way of life, only a religion with its rules and laws. Wherever you may be on the scale (even if you are not on it), how did you first think of God? As I mentioned previously,

I grew up in the church as that was just what we did in our family. I shared earlier of my experience of singing "Jesus Loves Me" in front of the church when I was five years old. I cannot say that I knew of what I was singing. I think I was convinced that "Jesus loved me" whatever that may have meant to me at the time. As I grew older, became a teenager and young adult I believe I knew less and less of the love of God and more and more of the condemnation of God. Looking back on those days, the seeming approach to God was always from a sense of guilt and wrongdoing.

One of the most well known Scriptures is John 3:16. I want us to look at that verse as well as John 3:17. "For God so loved the world that he gave his one and only Son, that whoever believes in him shall not perish but have eternal life. For God did not send his Son into the world to condemn the world, but to save the world through him." This admonition starts with the love *(gospelove)* of God through Jesus. We believe in Jesus because we believe and know He loves *(gospeloves)* us. He did not come to *condemn* the world, but to *save* the world. He saves the world on the basis of His *gospelove.* I mentioned earlier that we used to see people through the lens of condemnation or sin or whatever we may have called it. If we saw someone smoking or drinking a can of beer or heard them swearing, we immediately placed them in the condemnation box. Now, that might not have been so bad, but we did not think of them coming to Christ on the basis of His love, but on the basis of keeping the rules. We thought these were the rules of God, but some of them were the rules of the church and had little to do with God. They had to renounce these "condemnations", usually publicly, before the members of the congregation would truly accept them as "saved" or "born again". Often this would be an ongoing continual battle and we would somehow never get to the explanation of how much God loves *(gospeloves)* through Jesus. I shared the story of the friend of my parents who through the love of Jesus in them led him to the altar of repentance. Remember, the first word from the pastor was about the condemnation, in this case smoking. What if the pastor had been able to say that Jesus loves you and He is going to help you in your every, ordinary life to follow HIm. As I reflect on my parents and LaVonna's parents I realize that they influenced people around them with the love of Jesus. It was not a "program" or "ministry" of the church, but just came from their own *gospelove* relationship with Jesus.

What if we, especially those who may be part of a church, just began to follow Jesus. Follow His commands and His commission to love God with all, love their neighbors, love their enemies, and start sowing seeds everywhere they went in their ordinary, everyday lives. Can we believe that God will do what He says He will do? Do we really believe the words of Jesus when He says, "No one can come to me unless the Father who sent me draws them?" (John 6:44) "For my Father's will is that everyone who looks to the Son and believes in him shall have eternal life, and I will raise them up at the last day." (John 6:40) So, what about the condemnation? Many believe that if we love *(gospelove)* first, then anything goes and we do not stand for anything. In other words, our *unconditional* love is a license to do whatever you want to do, with no condemnation, punishment, or repentance. Do we not believe the words of Jesus to his disciples just before He went to the cross in John 16:8-11, "When he (the Holy Spirit) comes, he will prove (convince or convict) the world to be in the wrong about sin and righteousness and judgment: about sin, because people do not believe in me; about righteousness, because I am going to the Father, where you can see me no longer; and about judgment, because the prince of this world now stands condemned?" When the *gospelove* of Jesus is being lived out by His people, the conviction of the Holy Spirit comes upon those who are being *gospeloved* and drawn by the Father. In my experience, many of us pastors and church leaders have usurped the role of the Holy

Spirit and have tried to bring the conviction by our own fleshly and sometimes manipulative means.

My dad had started a business in what was then one of the first "strip malls". The shop next to him was a barbershop and two young barbers had moved from southern California (we were in Northern California) and started their business. As time went, my parents developed a friendship with one of the barbers and his young family. Since they did not have any family in the area, my parents, through the *gospelove* of Jesus, became friends, parents, and grandparents to their young children. They would often go stay with the children if the parents needed to go somewhere and my mom, who was an amazing cook, began to help the young wife in her cooking skills. I do not know what kind of conversations took place concerning their faith, church, etc., but one Sunday morning I saw them come into the sanctuary for the worship service. I was a teenager at the time and I was surprised to see them there. At the end of the sermon the pastor gave an invitation or what we called "an altar call" and invited people to come forward and to receive Christ as their Savior. To my surprise, they came forward and repented of their sins and placed their faith in Jesus. The man was invited to join the church softball team and he eagerly accepted the invitation and the next game he came to play on the team and his wife came as a spectator. It did not take but a few minutes until some of the ladies of the church who were there to watch the team begin to make their own judgments. One of those was that this new young female believer was wearing shorts that were deemed by them to "too" short and thus not appropriate for a "church" softball game. A few of them went to the pastor, who was there, and made their complaint along with a demand that he do something about it. Feeling the pressure, the pastor went to her and relayed the church ladies complaint and told her that she should not wear those kind of shorts in public. This new believer was humiliated, left in tears, and never came back to the church. What if the pastor had rather gone to her in *gospelove* and encouraged her that Jesus loved her and He would always be there to guide her in her new life of following Christ?

How do we bring this *gospelove* into our everyday, ordinary lives and sow the seeds in the world that we live in? As we consider how we can practically *gospelove* our world, we need to begin where Paul began and we have looked at in 2 Corinthians 5:14, "For Christ's love compels us, because we are convinced that one died for all, and therefore all died. And he died for all, that those who live should no longer live for themselves but for him who died for them and was raised again." Our motivation clearly comes from the love of Jesus who died for us on the cross. It is at the cross where find conviction, humility, and *gospelove!*

THE GOOD MEASURE PRINCIPLE

In Luke chapter 6, Jesus is teaching His disciples in what resembles an iteration of the Sermon on the Mount we find in Matthew 5-7. I believe these core values were shared often by Jesus, both to his disciples and to the crowds who came to hear him. So, in Luke 6:27-28 he says, "But to you who are listening I say : Love your enemies, do good to those who hate you, bless those who curse you, pray for those who mistreat you." I am not sure what his followers thought when they heard those words, but I would think there was a measure of shock and disbelief. Even though He had said that we are to "love our neighbor", which was also written in the Old Testament in Leviticus 19:18, "love your neighbor as yourself", I doubt if "enemies" entered the frame of their love. When Jesus told the parable of the good Samaritan (Luke 10:25-37), the expert in the law who had asked the question concerning the greatest commandment, now "wanted to justify himself, so he asked Jesus, 'And who is my neighbor?' " I believe this is also what the church in America has done as well. In almost every church, you can find something, somewhere that says something like "Love God and love your neighbor". So, we have ministries that are meant to "love our neighborhood" such as cleaning up a park or perhaps taking a few moments to try and help a homeless person. Now, these are good things and we should be doing these kinds of things in the name of Jesus, but we should not necessarily brand them as "loving your neighbor". Do we include "enemies" in those definitions and in those actions? Probably not. However, Jesus is very explicit and very clear in the verses we read in Luke 6:27-28. Are we honest enough and vulnerable at this point to ask Jesus, how do we do this?

When we defined *agape,* or *gospelove,* we realized that this is a command and not necessarily a feeling. This is an act of the will to be obedient to Jesus because He told us to *gospelove* our neighbors, which include enemies, as God has *gospeloved* us. He gave himself for us, particularly on the cross where "God made him (Christ) who had no sin to be sin for us, so that in him we might become the righteousness of God." (2 Corinthians 5:21) What often stops us is that when we come to an enemy, one who curses us, persecutes us, or mistreats us, we try and have good feelings toward them before we *gospelove* them. Then we feel like a hypocrite if we reach out to them in *gospelove* because we do not "feel" anything good toward them. Remember what Paul said in 2 Corinthians 5:16, "So from now on we regard no one from a worldly point of view. Though we once regarded Christ in this way, we do so no longer." We see these "enemies" as people for whom Christ died and while that might not change our feelings, it does change our perspective and we are able to *gospelove* them. Remember the golden rule, "Do to others as you would have them do to you." (Luke 6:31) It does not say "Feel about others as you would have them feel about you." I think we need to be reminded of what Jesus says next in this passage, "If you love those who love you, what credit is that to you? Even sinners love those who love them. And if you do good to those who are good to you, what credit is that to you?" (Luke 6:32-33) *Gospelove* is above and beyond our human capacity to love in our own strength. That is why it is so powerful in a world that does not know it or expect it or even how to respond to it.

What, then, is the good measure principle and how can it help or direct us in the life of obeying Jesus and becoming his ambassadors and witnesses to *gospelove*. In Luke 6:36 Jesus says, "Be merciful, just as your Father is merciful". In Matthew 5:7, Jesus says it this way, "Blessed are the merciful, for they will be shown mercy." *Mercy* and *grace* carry much of the same character and attribute of God and can be said to be the two sides of the same coin. *Mercy* is not receiving that which one deserves. Perhaps the most powerful statement of *mercy* is found in Romans 6:23, "For the wages of sin is death, but the gift (*mercy*) of God is eternal life in Christ Jesus our Lord." We see in Romans 3:23 that "all have sinned and fall short of the glory of God." Therefore, we are all separated from God and there is nothing we can do in our own strength or power to live up to the "glory of God." What we have earned through our "wages of sin" is death, eternal death apart from God. It is at the cross that we see the picture of mercy and grace most clearly. Jesus is dying in our place for our sin and He says to the Father, "Father forgive them (this includes us), for they do not know what they are doing." (Luke 23:34) We have sinned and the wages or consequences of sin is death, so we are receiving mercy from Jesus because we do not get what we deserve when we believe in Him and receive life rather than death. Grace is the fulfillment or completion of mercy as we not only do not get what we deserve, death (mercy), but He gives us life, eternal life, by His grace. In Romans 6:23, we can see mercy and grace come together, "For the wages of sin is death (what we have earned and it requires the mercy of God), but the gift of God is eternal life (grace, receiving something we did not earn) in Christ Jesus our Lord. It is at the cross where are most likely to be in a position to see our hopelessness and cry out for mercy. David, one of the most compelling figures in Scriptures, reveals the complete despair that sin has caused when he comes before the Lord, confronted by his own sin. A great leader of Israel, even a man characterized as a man after God's own heart, David is faced with his own sin of adultery with Bathsheba, causing the death of her husband, Uriah, and trying to cover up his sin with lies. So, he cries out in

Psalm 51:1-2, "Have *mercy* on me, O God, according to your unfailing love; according to your great compassion blot out my transgressions. Wash away all my iniquity and cleanse me from sin." Perhaps no one had a better pedigree to bring to the Lord and ask for His mercy, but David realized that it was not about him, but about the Lord.

So, how can we follow the direction of Jesus when He says, "Be merciful, just as your Father is merciful?" Our tendency here is to say that He is Jesus and He can do it, but I am not Jesus, so this is way beyond my reach. It is above and beyond our reach, except for one thing: *gospelove!* In the next few sentences Jesus explains to us the "good measure principle", which is summed up in verse 38, "For with the measure you use, it will be measured to you." Let's be clear, we cannot *gospelove* our neighbor and our enemy without showing and doing mercy. So, when someone hurts us, lies about us, resents us, is angry at us, treats us badly, persecutes us, and abuses us, how can we possible respond with mercy? Jesus starts with judgment: "Do not judge, and you will not be judged."(v. 37) The dictionary defines judgment as "the process of forming an opinion or evaluation by discerning and comparing." Our first reaction is to defend ourselves and say that we are not judgmental. However, we live in a world that thrives on judgment. Social media has amplified the process of opinions and comparing to a degree that we have not seen before. In order for us to *gospelove* someone or anyone, we must come to the cross and there remove our judgment on our neighbor or our enemy. How do we do that? We see them as a person for whom Jesus died and a person that He *gospeloves* and that he has a purpose for them in His kingdom. Now, we can argue with Jesus that they are not worth Him dying for, but remember what the Word says in Romans 5:8, "But God demonstrates his own love for us in this: While we (that includes you, me, your neighbor and your enemy) were still sinners (when the only hope we had was to cry out for God's mercy) Christ died for us." Here is the reality as expressed in v. 38, "For with the *measure* you use it will be *measured* to you." If we do not release people from our judgment, then we move ourselves out from under the mercy and grace of God and we are judged by God with the same standard we judge others.

Luke 6:37 goes on to say, "Do not condemn, and you will not be condemned." Now *condemn* is a strong word but it covers a lot of territory that is familiar to us. Included in this word *condemn* is to criticize, cut down, denigrate, defame, belittle, bad-mouth, deprecate, diminish, disparage, kiss off, put down, run down, talk down, trash, write off and others I am sure come to our mind. In my experience in the church, this word *condemn* and all that goes with it is the biggest reason there is constant conflict and disunity in the church. We are deceived by the enemy into thinking that most of it is just a little harmless gossip. According to Jesus, **there is no such thing as harmless gossip!** To be merciful will require that we are not a part of this *condemnation*, no matter what form it takes. Like many of my generation, I was hesitant to be a part of social media. However, during the pandemic we were limited in social contact, so I decided to try Facebook. At first, I enjoyed it as I was able to be in contact with people I had lost track of through the years. After a while, though, I began to see friends and ministerial colleagues post some things that to me were not really appropriate, at least not in the light of what Jesus is saying about the good measure principle. One day someone would post a wonderful Scripture that would be helpful, hopeful, and insightful. Then, tomorrow or the next day would come a post by the same person that would certainly fall into the category we have listed for *condemn*. These posts would assassinate character, mock, make fun of and all sorts of things that were just the opposite of the Scripture they had quoted in the previous post.

Finally, after a few months, I went off Facebook and have not looked at it again. So, am I *condemning* social media? Not at all; I just did not want to be a part of something that to me was not honoring the command of Christ to *gospelove*. Again, the measure we use, which in the context of *condemnation* is the opposite of *gospelove*, will be measured back to us. Have you ever said to someone or has someone said to you, "Can you keep a secret? I am not supposed to tell anyone, but I know I can trust you." What follows is usually a juicy bit of gossip that fits somewhere under the definitions of *condemnation*. I have come to the conclusion, and this is just me and my experience, is while there may be a person who can keep a confidence or secret, I have not met them yet. Jesus says what He means and means what He says. When He says, "do not condemn" I think He really means it and not as just another kind of rule or law "not to do". It is the opening of ourselves to be able to *gospelove* our neighbor (have you thought that this might include your spouse?) and our enemy, which the Father will use to draw them to Jesus.

The final part of Luke 6:27 is, "Forgive, and you will be forgiven." It may be that Jesus knew how difficult this would be, so He repeats it often to His disciples and followers. In what we often call "The Lord's Prayer" one of the petitions says, "And forgive us our debts, as we also have forgiven our debtors." (Matthew 6:12) Then at the conclusion of the prayer, He reiterates the point in v.14, "For if you forgive other people when they sin against you, your heavenly Father will also forgive you. But if you do not forgive others their sins, your Father will not forgive your sins." Paul, in his letter to the Ephesians wrote, "Be kind and compassionate to one another, forgiving each other, just as in Christ God forgave you." (Ephesians 4:32) To the Colossians he said, "Forgive as Christ forgave you." (Colossians 3:13) First, how completely does God forgive those who repent, according to Scripture? Psalm 103:3 says of the Lord, "who forgives all your sins." Then, in verse 12 we read, "as far as the east is from the west, so far has he removed our transgressions from us." Throughout the Bible we are made aware that the forgiveness that God gives through Christ is complete and covers all sin. John, in his first letter wrote in chapter one, verse seven, "But if we walk in the light, as he is in the light, we have fellowship with one another, and the blood of Jesus, his Son, purifies us from all sin." Then, in v. 9, writes "If we confess our sins, he is faithful and just and will forgive us our sins and purify us from all unrighteousness." Mark quotes Jesus in his gospel, "And when you stand praying, if you hold anything against anyone, forgive them, so that your Father in heaven may forgive you your sins." (Mark 12:25) In some ways these sayings by Jesus are troublesome because it sounds as if He is talking about works. If we forgive others, then God will forgive us. When Jesus forgave us from the cross, He offered forgiveness to all. It is here that the good measure principle takes effect. The grace of forgiveness has been given, but from what Jesus and his disciples are saying, the grace of forgiveness cannot be applied to us until we let go of the unforgivingness in our own hearts. So, how do we do this?

Forgiveness is releasing someone from our judgment. We are told from the time of Eve and Adam that the wages or consequences of sin is death. There is evidence all the way through the Bible, from Genesis through Revelation, that there will be judgment. The writer of Ecclesiastes sums it up when he says, "For God will bring every deed into judgment, including every hidden thing, whether it is good or evil." (Ecclesiastes 12:14) Our only hope is that through the *mercy* and *grace* of God through His Son, Jesus the Christ, we have been given forgiveness and pardon from our sin and the judgment upon us has been lifted. Now, Jesus says, we must *act* in the same way toward others. It appears the disciples had trouble with this concept as they had grown up with a religion said that if you could forgive someone up to seven times, you could wash your hands of them and consider that you had done your duty. So, now, in light of the teaching Jesus was giving, Peter asked, "Lord, how many times shall I forgive my brother or sister who sins against me? Up to seven times?" Jesus answers, "I tell you, not seven times, but seventy times seven." (Matthew 18:21-22) Jesus was actually saying that there is no end to the number of times you must forgive your brother or sister. Jesus then tells the parable of the unmerciful servant, which you can read in Matthew 18:23-35. It is the story of a servant to the king who owes the king a debt he cannot pay. The king ordered that the wife and children of the servant be sold as slaves to repay the debt. The servant cries out and asks for mercy and that he will somehow repay the debt. The king has mercy on him, *canceled the debt* and let him go. The servant left and then saw a fellow servant who owed him some money, so he demanded that the other servant pay him back. When he asked for mercy, the first servant gave him none but had him thrown into prison. When the king heard what this servant had done, he was furious and had the servant brought to him. The king said to him, "You wicked servant. I cancelled all that debt of yours because you begged me to. Shouldn't you have had mercy on your fellow servant just as I had on you?" The master handed him over to the jailers to have him tortured until he paid back the debt he owed. Jesus finishes this parable by saying, "This is how my heavenly Father will treat each of you unless you forgive your brother or sister from your heart."

In my observations, I believe that unforgivingness is the most frequently unconfessed sin of people in the church. It breeds anger, resentment, mistrust, suspicion and much other poison and toxicity. For certain, it is the killer of *gospelove.* The flow of the Holy Spirit of *gospelove* is blocked and what happens in our churches is that we develop a reservoir. However, it is not a reservoir where we can swim, boat, and fish, but one filled with toxicity, poison, and sin. We wonder why our churches are not fruitful and often do not portray what the Scriptures declare, "And we all, who with unveiled faces contemplate the Lord's glory, are being transformed into his image with ever increasing glory, which comes from the Lord, who is the Spirit." (2 Corinthians 3:18) How do we let someone who has hurt us be released from our judgment? It is not easy and the only place I know of to see clearly is at the cross. When I am truly before the cross of Jesus, see Him dying in my place, forgiving my sin, I can begin to let go. Again, our feelings betray us because even if we see what Jesus wants and recognize what He is doing for us, I still may not feel any different about that person whom I cannot seem to forgive. Also, many of us wait to act until that person comes to us to ask for forgiveness. Remember, in *gospelove* we must be proactive and intentional. Even if the other person never asks, that does not release us from giving forgiveness. So, the forgiveness we offer flows from what Jesus has and is doing for us and in us. It is as much or more for you than the offender. Yes, at times it will seem as if we are "letting them off the hook". That is not up to us, though. We have to trust Jesus with that person and what He does or does not do with them and for them. With the measure we use it will be measured back to us.

In Luke 6:38, Jesus says, "Give and it will be given to you. A good measure, pressed down, shaken together and running over, will be poured into your lap." I have read a number of books and listened to speakers at conferences describe this particular statement as a prosperity principle. They relate it to money or earthly goods. This happens often when we take Scripture out of a context and make it stand alone. This statement is in the context of the preceding sentences Jesus gave and also the one that follows. "With the measure you use, it will be measured to you." When we live a life full of mercy and grace and *gospelove* rather than judgment, condemnation, and unforgivingness, even more mercy, grace, and love will be poured out upon us, "pressed down, shaken together and running over." We will have a generous heart in all things, whether the things of this world (read Matthew 6) or the opening of the heart to the mercy, love, and grace of Jesus. *Gospelove* compels us and we will let the river flow into us and then out of us and through us Christ will change the world.

Gospelove and the good measure principle is not easy. It can be simple, but not easy. When our middle son, Kevin, was seven year old, he got sick over a weekend. He had a temperature and was feeling listless, which was always a telling clue with him, because he was constant energy. When Monday came, he was no better, so we called our pediatrician's office and gave them the symptoms and asked if we could get in to see the doctor. The best they could do was see him at 5:00P.M. His symptoms seemed to get worse throughout the day and it was finally time to see the doctor. When they called us in, the nurse was a friend of ours from high school and when she took one look at Kevin, she said I will be right back. She came right back in with the doctor and when he checked Kevin, he said to take him immediately to the emergency room and he would meet us there. He would call the ER doctor and tell him we were coming. They took him right in when we got there and after a few minutes they came out and said that he had pneumonia and his temperature had reached 105.9, but they were filling him full of antibiotics and he should start improving within 24 hours. They admitted him to the hospital and put him in ICU with an oxygen tent. LaVonna said she would stay there in the room and I went home to take care of our other two children. The next morning, I got the two kids to school and went to the hospital. Kevin did not look any better to me and LaVonna said the doctor should be in any minute. He then walked in and his first words almost made me collapse. He said, "Well, the good news is that he made it through the night." I had no idea his condition was that serious. For the next few days there seemed to be no improvement and everything they tried seemed to have little or no effect. The doctor shared with us his frustration as he had called any number of specialists and it seemed no one could put a finger on exactly what was wrong. They knew he had pneumonia but all the things they knew to do for that illness Kevin did not seem to be responding to. Near the end of the week, after more than five days in ICU, they had a cardiac/ thoracic specialist from Boston who was there for a couple of weeks, exam Kevin. After X-rays and ultrasounds, the doctor said he thought maybe the pneumonia was trapped by fluid in the lungs that seemed to be surrounding the pneumonia and the medicines and antibiotics were not getting to the actual illness. He suggested taking a large needle and going through the back and being directed through an ultrasound and maybe they could break up some of the fluid. I went with them so I could be there for support for Kevin and see what they were doing. They went in the first time with this giant needle and I could hardly stand what they were doing. They did not seem to find the fluid so they said they would try again, but after a couple of minutes when they had no success, I told them to stop, that was enough for my son to take. We did not know what to do. He was still in ICU in an oxygen tent and his eyes and demeanor were seemingly lifeless, though he was awake. When his teacher (second grade) from school came in, she was so shocked at how he looked that she needed to go out of the room and compose herself.

I found the chapel in the hospital and went in by myself, knelt at the altar that was there and wept and cried out to God. I came to the place, certainly not easily, to release Kevin into the arms of God and to whatever God wanted to do. Sunday came and LaVonna stayed in the hospital, but I went to the church and somehow was going to preach that Sunday morning. By the Spirit of God, I am sure, the district superintendent showed up unexpectedly (at least to me). Just as he arrived, LaVonna called from the hospital and said they needed me there as they had a procedure they wanted to try. Remembering the big needle, I was not sure, but I said I would be right there. I went in and told the district superintendent the situation and that he would be preaching. When I arrived at the hospital, the specialist and our pediatrician met with LaVonna and me. The specialist said they wanted to try a surgery where they would make an incision in his side and the doctor would put his hand in the side and try and reach the lung and see if he could penetrate the fluid with his finger. Hopefully, they could break down the pocket wall or membrane and they could put a drain that would let the fluid out of his body. I do not think they had ever tried something like that, but at this point we were all desperate. After an hour or so in surgery, the doctors came out and said that they had gotten to the fluid and it was not just one pocket, but several smaller ones and they had been able to break them down and they thought they were beginning to drain. By the next day, the drainage had gone well and Kevin began to improve. After another day or two, he was able to come home and he made a complete recovery.

I share that story because I think it can help illustrate how we can live out *gospelove* and the mercy, grace, and love of the good measure principle. Just imagine that the judgment, condemnation, unforgivingness that may be in your life is like the fluid that was trapped in my son's lung. It was doing all the damage, but it seemed nothing could reach it. So, we may pray to *gospelove* our neighbor and even our enemy, but our feelings and the situations get the better of us and we are not able to carry it out. However, if we come to the cross, see that Jesus died for us and that we must live for him, our prayer can be different. We can pray that the Holy Spirit of Jesus can be the surgeon and He can gently reach into our heart and break down the barriers we have put up. As we name the judgments, the condemnations, the inability to forgive, we give Him permission to begin to clean away the walls and let the toxic fluid begin to flow out of us. Instead, we can have the "spring of water welling up to eternal life." (John 4:14) Rivers of this living water can now flow out of us in the form of *gospelove* and Jesus, through us, can change the world. I remember a time in Africa when a team from a church in America had come to help us on a short term basis. When we went to church out in a rural village, I pointed out some of the children, from pastor's children to Aids orphans and explained that my wife, LaVonna, was leading a ministry of child sponsorship to be able to help these children so in need. He made a comment that how much good could that do since there were thousands and thousands of these children and we could only help a few and that it really would not make much difference in the world. I replied that it might not make much difference in the world, but it would make a world of difference to each child. As we share, express, and give the *gospelove* of Jesus to one person at a time, the Father will draw them to Jesus, one person at a time, our neighbors and our enemies. We are to be proactive and intentional and Jesus will build His church and God will produce the harvest. Let's go!

A TEMPLATE FOR LIVING OUT THE GOSPELOVE OF JESUS AND THE GOOD MEASURE PRINCIPLE.

One of the definitions for a template is "something that establishes or serves as a pattern." So, this is a pattern that will help you focus on and live out the *gospelove* of Jesus and good measure principle. It is a template and a pattern, so it gives you a framework, but it is not meant to be a rigid format, but one you adapt and make your own. I will be praying for everyone who has read this book. I do not know your name or what you look like or where you live, but through the Holy Spirit, I will lift you up in prayer every day. Know that you are loved!

1 CORINTHIANS 13 (MEMORIZE AND PRAY THROUGH)

YOU ARE LOVED BY GOD	John 15:9-17; 1 John 4:7-12
YOU ARE FORGIVEN BY GOD	Psalm 103:10,12-13, 1 John 1:9
LOVE YOUR GOD	Psalm 103:17-18, Matthew 22-34-38
LOVE YOUR NEIGHBOR	Psalm 103:17-18; Mark 12:28-31
LOVE YOUR ENEMY	Psalm 103:19-22, Luke 6:27-31
FOLLOW THE GOOD MEASURE PRINCIPLE	Luke 6:32-38

www.ingramcontent.com/pod-product-compliance
Lightning Source LLC
Chambersburg PA
CBHW061652120626
46550CB00003B/914